Alfred Jarry

Twayne's World Authors Series

Maxwell Smith, Editor

Guerry Professor of French, Emeritus
The University of Chattanooga
Former Visiting Professor in Modern Languages
The Florida State University

TWAS 681

ALFRED JARRY
(1873–1907)
Photograph by Nadar, 1896

Alfred Jarry

By Linda Klieger Stillman

Georgetown University

Twayne Publishers • *Boston*

Alfred Jarry

Linda Klieger Stillman

Copyright © 1983 by G. K. Hall & Company
All Rights Reserved
Published by Twayne Publishers
A Division of G. K. Hall & Company
70 Lincoln Street
Boston, Massachusetts 02111

Book Production by Marne B. Sultz
Book Design by Barbara Anderson

Printed on permanent/durable acid-free
paper and bound in The United States
of America.

Library of Congress Cataloging in Publication Data

Stillman, Linda Klieger.
   Alfred Jarry.

   (Twayne's world authors series: TWAS 681)
   Bibliography: p. 159
   Includes index.
   1. Jarry, Alfred, 1873–1907—Criticism and
interpretation.   I. Title.   II. Series.
PQ2619.A65Z78 1983   842'.8   82–15861
ISBN 0–8057–6528–X

Contents

About the Author
Preface
Chronology

Chapter One
The Man and the Mask (1873–1907)   1

Chapter Two
Pataphysically Speaking . . .   16

Chapter Three
Long Live the King: Ubu   43

Chapter Four
Double or Nothing   60

Chapter Five
Love   92

Chapter Six
Progeny and Premonition   124

Chapter Seven
Conclusion   139

Notes and References   149
Selected Bibliography   159
Index   162

About the Author

Since 1979, Linda Stillman has been teaching in the French Department of Georgetown University. She has spoken and published on Adamov, Sartre, Barthes, Yourcenar, Dubillard, and Jarry. Her *La Théâtralité dans l'oeuvre d'Alfred Jarry* appeared in 1980. Dr. Stillman is a *membre honorifique* of the *Collège de Pataphysique* and a member of the *Société des Amis d'Alfred Jarry.*

Preface

Although Alfred Jarry has rightfully been declared the equal of Baudelaire, Rimbaud, Lautréamont, Sade, and Roussel, a meager number of articles and chapters of books, a handful of doctoral dissertations, and only three book-length critical studies (two treating a specific work and one his dramaturgy) have appeared to date in the English language. In France, Jarry has fared better, but it was not until 1948 that his "complete works" were published, in an incomplete edition. During the 1960s the Ubu plays and Jarry's critical essays on dramaturgy were made accessible to the general public by the publication in a paperback edition of *Tout Ubu*. Still, however, Jarry was known primarily, if not exclusively, as the "father of the Theater of the Absurd" and remained unknown in the gamut of his creative powers as novelist, poet, dramatic theorist, art critic, and, indeed, playwright of any but the Ubu texts.

The turning point in Jarry studies came, in 1972, with the publication of the first volume of his complete works (more "complete" than the 1948 version) by Gallimard, edited by Michel Arrivé, who that same year published a semiotic study of "Jarry's languages." But here, again, more than half of the analysis focuses on dramatic works. The following two years brought Henri Béhar's study of Jarry's theater, the compendious first volume of Noël Arnaud's biographical-critical study (which goes beyond Jarry's theater), and the first general critical study by François Caradec.

This brief survey in no way means to underestimate the importance of Jarry's dramatic works or of the critical studies they have provoked. *Ubu Roi* [King Ubu] is alive and well, staged by Peter Brook in New York as recently as May 1980. Jarry continues to challenge our ideas about theater's function and components. But Jarry's genius and talent far surpass that portion of his writings—about one-third of this total output—devoted to Ubu. This book will be a first step toward bringing Jarry's other texts out of the dark and into the public domain: they are daring and enigmatic works of art. While his theater has received critical attention, and Jarry himself has become the notorious subject of countless anecdotes, his other important writings have been largely consigned to obscurity. A primary goal of this study is to help the reader of Jarry navigate the private world of a serious and meaningful life-work. It is a work whose creative force far exceeds the infamous Ubu character, beyond which only very few have ventured.

Lacking the propulsion of narrative, i.e., a "plot" operating on and in time, these works cannot be analyzed in a traditional way. Because the texts essentially constitute a structural mapping of a "psychic set" or unconscious networks of images, plot summaries are, even where possible, unimportant. Therefore, this study concentrates on images, symbols, and signs: their significance and their inter-relationships. The critical strategy is to take an emblematic, overlaid, concentrated text and reorganize its components so that the reader may recuperate the text's coherence and knowledge.

All of Jarry's major works are considered, including *La Dragonne* [The She-Dragoon], a work he never completed but plans for which he dictated to his sister during his terminal illness. *La Chandelle verte* [The Green Candle], a compilation of articles, is not treated as a whole, but selections are mentioned in reference to other works. Jarry's juvenilia, collected under the title *Ontogénie* [Ontogenesis], are analyzed only in terms of germinal forms of mature works and not as independent objects of study. Works such as *Les Minutes de sable mémorial* and *L'Amour en visites* [Love Goes Visiting] which are not susceptible to discussion as a whole have been dismembered and redistributed under pertinent topics of analysis. A few "mirlitonesque" works (*Pantagruel, La Papesse Jeanne* [Pope Jean], and *Le Moutardier du Pape* [The Pope's Mustard Maker]) have been omitted owing to space limitations in this edition. They are represented, though, by *L'Objet aimé* [The Beloved Object].

Jarry wrote at a critical moment in the history of man and of literature: the inauguration of what we now call the "modern age." He seems to have had a gift for intuiting and establishing a new spirit, a new consciousness, and a new discourse. At the same time, his works speak to the collective unconscious of all people.

I would like to acknowledge permission granted by *Sub-Stance* and the University of Wisconsin Press to use some of the material included in my article "Modern Narrative Techniques: Jarry, the Pre-Text."

My thanks to Noël Arnaud for generously making available a collection of Jarry photographs and for inviting me to speak at the "Colloque Jarry" in Cerisy-la-Salle, to Michel Arrivé for his insights and encouragement, to Joan Stewart for her attentive reading of the manuscript, and to Robert, who long ago gave me the Pléiade *Jarry* for Valentine's Day.

Linda Klieger Stillman

Georgetown University

Chronology

1873   Birth of Alfred-Henry Jarry in Laval (Mayenne) on 8 September, Feast of the Nativity of the Holy Virgin.

1879   Jarry's mother Caroline, née Quernest, leaves her husband, Anselme, and moves with her son and his older sister Charlotte to Saint-Brieuc; Jarry enters the *lycée*.

1886–1888   Writes first "literary" texts, later collected as *Ontogénie*.

1888   Mme Jarry and her children move to Rennes; Alfred enters the Rennes *lycée* in October; he and his friends stage *Les Polonais* (an early form of *Ubu Roi*) and *Onésime ou les Tribulations de Priou* (the original version of *Ubu Cocu*) at their marionette theater.

1891   Jarry enters the Lycée Henri IV in Paris to prepare for the competitive exam for acceptance to the Ecole Normale Supérieure.

1893   Jarry is very ill; publication of "Guignol"; death of Mme Jarry in Paris, where she had come to care for her son; Jarry begins to attend the Tuesday gatherings of the *Mercure de France* (sponsored by Alfred Vallette and Rachilde), alternating with Mallarmé's "Tuesdays."

1894   Becomes friends with Léon-Paul Fargue; "Etre et Vivre," "Visions actuelles et futures," and "Haldernablou" published; Jarry, registered for the fourth time, does not show up for the E.N.S. entrance exam; *Minutes de sable mémorial* published (incorporates "Haldernablou" and "Guignol"); begins military service in Laval.

1895   Break between Jarry and Fargue; death of Jarry's father in Laval; *César-Antechrist* published as a complete play.

1896   "Le Vieux de la Montagne," *Ubu Roi*, "De l'inutilité du théâtre au théâtre," and "L'Autre Alceste" published; performance of *Ubu Roi* at the *Théâtre de l'Oeuvre*, 10 December.

1897   "Questions de théâtre" and *Les Jours et les Nuits* published.

1898   Jarry and friends rent villa in Corbeil, called the "Phalanstère"; finishes *Gestes et opinions du Docteur Faustroll, pataphysicien; L'Amour en visites*, chapters 6 and 10 through 25 of *Faustroll*, and *Le Petit Almanach* published; attends Mallarmé's funeral; moves back to Paris; performance of *Ubu Roi* at the *Théâtre des Pantins* by Pierre Bonnard's marionettes.

1899   "Commentaire pour servir à la construction pratique de la machine à explorer le temps," *L'Amour absolu, Ubu Enchaîné*, and *Messaline* (in installments) published.

1901   A satirical chronicle, *Almanach illustré du Père Ubu*, published; first "Spéculation" article appears in *La Revue blanche* (the periodical had published Jarry's articles since 1896); first performance of marionette play *Ubu sur la Butte* (shortened version, with songs, of *Ubu Roi*); last "Spéculation" published: series replaced by "Gestes."

1902   *Le Surmâle* published; lectures on puppets in Brussels; cessation of "Gestes."

1903   "Périples de la littérature et de l'art" and "La Bataille de Morsang" (a portion of *La Dragonne*) published; articles published in *L'Oeil*; begins correspondence with Apollinaire.

1904   Travel between Paris and Grand-Lemps, where he works on *Pantagruel;* "Fantaisie parisienne" published in *Le Figaro*.

1905   Travels to Brittany; very ill and without money during the winter; begins work with Dr. Saltas on translation of *La Papesse Jeanne;* reworks *La Dragonne;* asks Claude Terrasse to return manuscript of *L'Objet aimé.*

1906   *Par la Taille* published: had been ready since 1900; *Ubu sur la Butte* published; gravely ill, in Laval, dictates plan of *La Dragonne* to his sister; from May 1906–October 1907 travels between Paris and Brittany.

1907   Returns to Paris 7 October; found semiconscious in his apartment by friends 29 October; died at 4:15 PM on 1 November, All Saints Day; funeral service 3 November at Saint-Sulpice; burial at Bagneux Cemetery; his grave disappeared a few years later; *Le Moutardier du Pape.*

Posthumous publications:

1908   *La Papesse Jeanne.*

1909   *L'Objet aimé.*

1911   *Pantagruel, Gestes et opinions du Docteur Faustroll, pataphysicien, roman néo-scientifique, suivi de Spéculations.*

1927   *Les Silènes.*

1943   *La Dragonne.*

1944   *Ubu cocu.*

1948   *Oeuvres poétiques complètes.*

1964   *Saint-Brieuc des Choux.*

1974   *Le Manoir enchanté (et quatre autres oeuvres inédites).*

Chapter One
The Man and the Mask (1873–1907)

His final request—for a toothpick—satisfied, Alfred Jarry died at the age of thirty-four. Although he was clinically afflicted with meningeal tuberculosis, his death, on 1 November 1907, was precipitated by a determined course of exhaustion, malnutrition, and drink. He died as eccentrically as he had lived, systematically inserting the absurd and the hallucinatory into daily life. The infamous toothpick symbolizes Jarry's desire to blend life with art. The most ordinary object suddenly acquired a new status: it was infused with power, became unconventional. It is absolutely appropriate that the lowly toothpick somehow magically permitted Jarry's passage into the realm of the eternal dream. The absurd deathbed toothpick, in its "complex simplicity,"[1] epitomizes a life devoted to cultivating the hallucination, a life predictably and yet startlingly ended on All Saints Day.

Childhood: 1873–1888

In a rather provincial bourgeois setting in Laval, Mayenne, Caroline Quernest Jarry gave birth to Alfred Henry on 8 September 1873. That propitious year would also witness the publishing of Tristan Corbière's *Les Amours jaunes* and Rimbaud's *Une Saison en enfer*. In 1873, at the start of the Third Republic, who could have guessed an event that would change the course of the avant-garde had taken place at the home of Anselme Jarry, that unsuccessful traveling salesman and disdained husband? Taking his cue from his mother, a woman—not unlike Emma Bovary—given to grandiose pretensions and aspirations, Alfred denied his

1

diligent mild-mannered father all respect. His friend Rachilde
recounts:

"Our father," he told me one day without the slightest hint of emotion,
"was a totally unimportant fellow, what's known as a regular guy. He
undoubtedly made our older sister, a girl of the 1830s who likes to put
ribbons in her hair, but he cannot have participated much in the
confection of our precious self."[2]

Once his mother moved (in 1878) with him and his sister Charlotte to her father's house in Saint-Brieuc, Alfred saw little of his
father. Like his mother, he would be devoured by his obsessions
and eccentricities. It is not surprising to learn that the Quernest
family harbored strains of emotional instability and downright
insanity.

During the school year 1885–86 he wrote the first of his
schoolboy works, collectively entitled *Ontogénie* [Ontogenesis].
The following two years again proved fertile for more skits and
a proliferation of poems obviously patterned in the style of Victor
Hugo, whose sumptuous funeral—in May 1885—impassioned
all of Paris and heralded a new era in French Letters. With
compulsive fervor, Jarry renewed his imitation of Hugo in the
spring of 1888, composing poems of lugubrious content. It was
here, in Saint-Brieuc, on the coast of Brittany, that Jarry shrewdly
observed the mores of his neighbors and became versed in Celtic
lore. His portrayal of provincial life would be stinging; his knowledge of Celtic tradition would provide the atmosphere and décor
for many of his works.

Lycée Years in Rennes: 1888–1891

By the time Madame Jarry moved with her children to Rennes,
her son had won more than twenty prizes for scholastic achieve-
ment in fields from French, Greek, Latin, English, and German
to mathematics, physical sciences, and geography. The wide scope
of information assimilated by this above-average student would
serve him constantly in his fiction. Not only did he master the
teachings of the Ancients and the French classics, but he kept

abreast of the latest literary and scientific accomplishments of his day.

Monsieur Hébert's physics class at the Lycée provided the crucible for Jarry's savage creativity. Several generations of students had already maligned the obese, fumbling man by means of a collection of stories which grew to epic proportions. Jarry spiritedly participated in the cruel antics and formulated new adventures for the unfortunate Hébert. The Professor's name varied from Père Heb, to P.H., to Ebouille, to Ebé: the model from which Jarry fashioned the future Ubu, whose "science of physics" creates, destroys, and transforms at will. Unlike the diminutive Jarry, Père Heb's girth was his trademark.

Before long, Jarry had usurped leadership and organized a performance of *Les Polonais* [The Poles], so titled since it recounts the exploits of P.H. as King of Poland. Jarry's close friend Henri Morin—whose older brother Charles had authored the play about three years prior to its staging by the makeshift *Théâtre des Phynances*—played the ignominious King. Only eight years hence, the momentous *Ubu Roi* [King Ubu] rocked the Parisian literary scene. In the years to come, Jarry embellished and reworked the basic legend in light of quickly maturing philosophical, psychological, and aesthetic ends. Whether or not Jarry was the original author of the classroom saga matters little and alters neither our respect for his cleverness nor his artistry.

Paris—Entering the Scene: 1891–1894

Jarry earned the first part of the baccalaureate in 1889 and the second the following year. He finally opted for the Ecole Normale over the Ecole Polytechnique, and in 1891 he left for Paris to prepare at the Lycée Henri IV for the entrance exams. Paris was his elixir and his poison. The seventeen-year-old Jarry entered a milieu which nurtured the Symbolists, acclaimed the avant-garde productions of Lugné-Poe's Théâtre de l'Oeuvre, sympathized with the anarchists, and celebrated the occult. He brought with him his decided taste for Shakespeare, Poe, Rabelais, the Classics, and the occult sciences of heraldry and the Cabala. His professor in Rennes had taught the—as yet untranslated—heretical and prophetic theories of Nietzsche. At school in Paris he heard Henri Bergson's innovative ideas on comedy. Jarry's world was fairly swirling with all types of stimulation; he even became a fanatic practitioner of the latest means of transport: the bicycle. His writings utilize all of the input.

Amid the tumult, Jarry's sole desire was to astonish the common crowd. He began by his appearance. His intimate friend and fellow *lycéen* Léon-Paul Fargue described his sensational attire. "At that time Jarry sported a stovepipe hat, undoubtedly purchased in the provinces, whose dome was incredibly tall, a veritable observatory and a hooded cape that fell all the way to his heels."[3] The ferocious mockery with which Jarry approached life manifested itself in his physical presence. He would be dubbed "the Indian" because of his gaucho pants and greased hair. Eventually, the nonconformist was seen only in the uniform of a confirmed cyclist. The poet Henri de Régnier described Jarry, the newcomer to the Tuesday gatherings of Symbolists sponsored by the *Mercure de France:*

[A] short stocky man, with a large head and broad shoulders, planted on bowlegs. In a pale face, with fine contracted features and a thin brown moustache, brilliant eyes shone with a metallic glare. At the bottom of knee-breeches, calves ringed in garters ended in feet shod in rubber-soled shoes. . . . His pockets bulged with cycling tools, among which one could see the butt of an old revolver, at once sordid and disquieting.[4]

He adds sympathetically,

Those who knew him say that behind this loathsome appearance was a boy who was stubborn, timid, proud, amazing, but good-natured, candid in his cynicism, ferociously independent, and rigorously honest.[5]

Between 1891 and 1893, when he renounced the world of the classroom in favor of the life of cafés and literary soirées, Jarry fell gravely ill and, in addition, suffered the death of his beloved mother. Nevertheless, he managed to launch his literary career, winning several poetry and prose contests which led, in 1893, to his first publications. His talent was immediately recognized by the likes of Marcel Schwob, editor of the literary supplement of *L'Echo de Paris,* and Schwob's coworkers Octave Mirbeau and Catulle Mendès. Soon he was alternating between attending Mallarmé's famous Tuesday gatherings—occasionally having the master's undivided attention after hours—and those held by Alfred Vallette, editor of the *Mercure de France,* and his wife, Rachilde, a novelist. The Vallettes were Jarry's guardian angels: they nurtured him professionally, published his writings, and tended to his needs during his final years of illness and poverty. At the *Mercure,* Jarry mixed with the entire loosely knit brotherhood of Symbolists, including Franc-Nohain, Pierre Louys, Gustave Kahn, and some young upstarts such as Paul Valéry and André Gide. Jarry established himself with alacrity in these Parisian literary circles as much by the theatrical space he always created as by what he wrote.

His apartment, at 78 boulevard de Port-Royal (bordering the Latin Quarter and Montparnasse), constituted the setting for what we might today call "living theater." Jarry referred to it with affectionate mockery as the "Calvaire du Trucidé," which means, colloquially, "Murdered Man's Calvary." Some who were invited described it as

a funereal room, with closed shutters, the walls hung with black cloth; skeletons, skulls, and tibias completed the décor, illuminated by a lamp draped with crepe and by a nightlight lit in a skull; on a table a small owl keeps watch near an open Bible. The only error of mise en scène: inadvertently, Jarry left a pair of dumb-bells lying in a corner.[6]

These trappings created the perfect atmosphere in which to mystify his friends. Jarry performed macabre one-man shows to their baffled amusement, an owl often perched on his fist. An apt pet for such a bizarre man, the owl—which Jarry whimsically called *le zibou*—pleased by its nocturnal habits, traditional connotation of evil, and ridiculous beak.

Paris—A Developing Career: 1894–1896

Professionally, the year 1894 was a red-letter one. Three important texts were published and, with his friend Rémy de Gourmont, Jarry founded a lavish pictorial review, *L'Ymagier*. He initiated a correspondence with the avant-garde director Lugné-Poe, who would not only employ Jarry, but whose theater would produce *King Ubu*. In the spring of that year *L'Art littéraire* published a short theoretical work, *Etre et Vivre* [To Be and to Live], in which Jarry considers the pros and cons of "Being" as opposed to "Living": it is an essential manual of Jarry's philosophy.

The future "Acte prologal" of *César-Antechrist* [Caesar-Antichrist] appeared in the summer issue, under the name "l'Acte unique." In the heraldic play *Caesar-Antichrist*, published in its entirety the following year, Jarry discloses the profound meaning of Ubu as the Antichrist on earth. He shattered any illusion that Ubu was simply the grotesque clown or the political buffoon many assumed him to be. This work clearly points to another facet of Jarry's writing, and one crucial to its comprehension: *intertextuality*. Jarry's works only become cohesive and understandable when read as a network of interconnecting passages. The case of Ubu is illustrative. It was in "Guignol" [Puppet Show] (the entry that won the prize from *L'Echo de Paris*'s literary supplement in 1893 for the best prose work by a young writer) that Ubu made his first appearance as Ubu, and Père Heb receded forevermore into the annals of *lycée* history. Under his new mantle, Monsieur Ubu introduced his science of Pataphysics—which would surface again full blown in the Ubu cycle (King, Cuckolded, Enchained) and, later, in the novels *Gestes et opinions du docteur Faustroll, pataphysicien* [Exploits and Opinions of Doctor Faustroll, Pataphysician] and *Les Jours et les Nuits* [Days and Nights]. Ubu's Conscience, habitually carried in a suitcase, also has a role in "Puppet Show." This piece forms part of Jarry's first book, *Les Minutes de sable mémorial*,[7] a dense, hybrid work published in September 1894 by the *Mercure de France*. Another key piece included in this volume, *Haldernablou*—the title combines the names of the characters, the Duke Haldern and the page

Ablou—is reminiscent of Symbolism and is stylistically at antipodes with the Ubu fragments.

Sections of *Les Minutes de sable mémorial* led the Surrealists to claim Jarry as a precursor. "Opium," for example, anticipated their work. Intertextually, "Opium," along with certain elements of *Haldernablou*, predate *Days and Nights*—Jarry's novel superficially about his military stint. His "astral" self and his "terrestrial" self part ways: the first goes exploring areas which remind one of a collage, juxtaposing unlikely images. *Les Minutes de sable mémorial* clearly provides the meeting ground for the variety of Jarry's styles and genres. Beneath this apparent diversity, Jarry's doctrine of Pataphysics and the projection of his own multiple personalities into literature persist; the reader, then, has the job of fusing together what seems at first to be a hodgepodge of poetry, drama, and prose, written at that pivotal moment in the history of French Letters when the twentieth century was letting its birth wail be heard full force. Themes dominate here that will be developed on a larger scale in future works, especially those of sexual inversion and the quest for the absolute in all spheres: mental, physical, and spiritual. Jarry expressed these concerns in the form, alternatingly, of opaque, fiercely personal language and of explosive, grotesque, "ubuesque" banter.

The enterprise of publishing *L'Ymagier* during this period was made possible by a small inheritance Jarry received. Jarry and Gourmont, according to Jarry's biographer Noël Arnaud,

collected valuable antique engravings, sollicited and obtained original works from artist friends, wrote appropriate texts to set the tone for this publication that wanted to be incomparable, and would be, and that would soon be imitated by everyone, without anyone—except Jarry himself—ever equaling it.[8]

For five issues, Jarry worked at collecting prints of primitive art, engravings by Dürer, and woodcuts he and his co-editor produced themselves. Subsequent to a quarrel with Gourmont, involving Gourmont's elderly, lecherous mistress, Berthes de Courrière—publicly ridiculed by the untamed sarcasm of Jarry in "Chez la Vieille Dame"—the two men split up. On his own in 1896,

Jarry founded the rival magazine *Perhinderion;* his extravagant taste in printing quickly cost him his inheritance. The review expired after two issues.

Jarry had, in the meantime, moved to another one of his famous lodgings, this time a rather fancy apartment on the boulevard Saint-Germain. There he set up a marionette theater with which to delight his friends. He was, however, called up for military service, in November 1894, and left for his regiment in Laval—having been refused permission to join recruits in Paris. It was from the barracks that he continued to direct *L'Ymagier.*

Needless to say, Jarry proved to be less than the ideal soldier. In his comically ill-fitting uniform, his hair down to his bohemian shoulders, he infuriated his superiors by politely pointing out the absurdity of their exercises. When he purposefully drank a good swig of acid—a stunt ending in hospitalization—the troops bid him a relieved farewell. A few months later, on 14 December 1895, he prematurely became a civilian once again, taking with him a vast fund of experience from which to create the skeleton structure of *Days and Nights,* appropriately subtitled "novel of a deserter."

Paris—Fame but not Fortune: 1896

During this banner year in his meteoric career, Jarry had four more articles published, became Lugné-Poe's hard-working secretary at the Théâtre de l'Oeuvre, and sojourned in Holland at the homes of the poet Gustave Kahn and the artist Léonard Sarlius. He was befriended by Oscar Wilde's cohort Lord Douglas and the actress Fanny Zaessinger, among others. *King Ubu* was published in June. But the highlight of the year came in December, with the premiere of the now-infamous play.

By that time, Jarry had transformed himself into the character he invented. It is difficult at best to surmise what Alfred Jarry was "really" like. Anecdotes abound. When refused seating in the orchestra, he insisted in a stage whisper—as the curtain rose on the opera—"I don't see why they allow the audience in the first three rows to come in carrying musical instruments."[9] He was sarcastic but engaging. He ordered a complete dinner in reverse, beginning with brandy and ending with soup; he then ordered a small glass of red ink into which he dipped a piece of sugar—to be eaten with great relish—without deigning to notice the bewilderment of the restaurateur.[10] In a world he considered profoundly mediocre, he pushed his own existence to the absurd. By fanatically exercising his individual freedom, he reached the borders of dementia.

No doubt his calculated overindulgence in drink helped him along. The misogynist's only female friend, Rachilde, recounts:

Jarry began the day by imbibing two liters of white wine, three absinthes spaced between 10:00 AM and noon; then, at lunch, he washed down his fish or his steak with red or white wine, alternating with more absinthes. In the afternoon, a few cups of coffee fortified with brandy or spirits of which I forget the names; then, at dinner, after, of course, other apéritifs, he could still tolerate at least two bottles of any vintage, of good or bad quality. However, I never saw him really drunk, except once when I aimed at him with his own revolver, which sobered him up immediately. Personally drinking nothing but absolutely pure water, it was me whom Jarry considered a frightful phenomenon: "You're poisoning yourself, Ma-da-me," he explained to me, as seriously as could be. "Water contains, in suspension, all the bacteria of heaven and earth, and your sweets, which form your main nourishment, are spirits in a rudimentary state that intoxicate in a completely different way than do spirits expediently purged of all their harmfulness by fermentation."[11]

Drinking was a necessary ritual in his effort to transform his waking life into a continued hallucination or dream.. Existence became literary: Jarry enclosed himself inside Ubu and the unconscious rumblings of Jarry's violated self became concrete. The man and the character fused into a walking nightmare. Jarry became Ubu: speech, demeanor, behavior, and all. Reflecting upon his particularly outlandish antics, Jarry was known to compare the beauty of the experience to literature, saying, "N'est-ce pas que c'était bien comme littérature?"

Perhaps because he devoted himself to being another, or the Other, Jarry seemed unable to form any lasting romantic bonds. Once he broke with his intimate friend Léon-Paul Fargue, it is probable that he established no new relationships. Indeed, he appeared incapable of loving anyone after the death of his cherished mother. Once she was gone, his life lost its fragile equilibrium. Evidence of his homosexual tendency and aversion for women fills his writings. Although he portrays males as couples and women as courtesans, he describes the gamut of sexual experience. Friends remember his boastful indulgence in brothels as early as his years in the Lycée of Rennes. [12] And yet, even the penchant for homosexual love evident in his works is fraught with brooding frustration, violence, and finally death as the only possible outcome. For Jarry, sex always leads to the need for purification through murder, if it is not the actual cause of death itself. Even when purely mechanical, as in *Le Surmâle* [The Supermale], the sex act proves lethal.

Alcoholism was his faith, absolute purity his goal. And steadily, Ubu gnawed away at Jarry, speaking through his puppeteer in flat, staccato syllables. Bombastic utterances and stylized gestures completed the characterization. Once Ubu was monstrously incarnated on the planks—to mixed but tempestuous reviews— Jarry gave himself with vigor to perfecting his consubstantiality with his character. Alfred Jarry became a legend: the personification of the precocious, eccentric man of letters, possessed by some glacial inner demon driving him to increasingly disconcerting excesses. Although—and perhaps because—scarred by illness, wine, and devastating finances, his capacity for self-mockery through self-theatricalization never wavered.

Imitating *le parler Ubu* (Jarry/Ubu's peculiar diction) became fashionable in Parisian literary circles. Jarry fascinated one and all by resolutely playing the role of *enfant terrible,* wearing Rachilde's yellow shoes to Mallarmé's funeral, painting a black tie on the paper shirt he donned for an evening at the opera, deliberately surrounding himself with the most dramatic settings.

His living quarters as of November 1897 were no exception. At 7, rue Cassette, on the second and a half floor, his squalid room was respectfully christened "Our Great Chasublerie" in honor of a manufacturer of ecclesiastical vestments—his neighbor a half-floor below. This miniature apartment suited the short, bowlegged Jarry to a tee. Although even he accumulated plaster dust in his hair, unlike most of his guests he could stand erect under the low ceiling. Apollinaire's priceless description of Jarry's hovel focuses on a key word: reduction. The floor was a half-floor; the room a half-room; the only furnishing a bed; the bed lacking its legs; the writing table merely the floor Jarry used while flat on his stomach. Rousseau's portrait of Jarry that adorned the wall was in tatters. Scattered about, a few cheap volumes constituted the "library." Old bottles, back issues of magazines, and his current manuscript coexisted in disorder. An oversized stone phallus covered with a violet skullcap completed the interior. Jarry covered the artifact since it had once frightened a certain lady of letters. To her query "Is it a cast?" Jarry demurely countered, "No. It's a reduction."[13]

The Phalanstère—Life in the Country: 1897–1900

Despite physical hardships, new manuscripts regularly emerged: *Days and Nights,* "Questions about Theater," and *L'Amour en visites* [Love Goes Visiting] in 1897; *Faustroll,* parts of *Pantagruel,* and *Par la taille* in 1898. Père Ubu—as Jarry's friends knew him—wrote equally well at the Chasublerie or at the royal country domain, the Phalanstère. Rather than risk the salutary effect of life in this delightful villa rented by the Vallettes in Seine-et-Oise, he left the company of his hosts, A. F. Hérold, Marcel Collière, and Pierre Quillard, to set up shop nearby, in an abandoned mule stable on the banks of the Seine at Coudray. There he recreated the miserable conditions in which his role of intellectual debauchee flourished. Because of the moist dirt floor, Jarry suspended his bed from the ceiling. He also hung his bicycle in his "Studio," so that the tires might escape attack by the rats. Amid fishheads and debris from his drinking, he entertained his friends.

Toward the end of his life, Jarry embarked upon a career as a landowner. With all the pomp worthy of Père Ubu, he commissioned a "medieval dungeon" on his plot near the villa the Vallettes had purchased. In defiance of logic, of course, he named the four-postered shanty the "tripod."[14] His escapades at his (never paid for) riverside retreat are reported to be some of his most outrageous. All of his regal equipment was primed: canoe, fishing rod, pistol, and bicycle. In keeping with the periphrastic style he affected, Père Ubu pompously called his two-wheeler "that which rolls." In an untranslatable pun, André Bréton suggested (in his *Anthologie de l'humour noir*) that Jarry be called *celui qui révolver,* in mock tribute to the firearms he used to enhance his reputation.[15] Jarry considered his bicycle an extension of his own body, even referring to his knee—after a minor accident—as the "left pedal."[16] He possessed a remarkable faculty for baffling and infuriating those less prone to irony. One summer day, a panicky mother complained to her tenant Rachilde that Jarry risked her children's lives by shooting bottles arranged against her vulnerable garden wall. Unperturbed, as usual, Père Ubu graciously assured the woman that he would gladly make some new ones with her should any be killed inadvertently. As for his other accoutrements, if Jarry disdained drinking water in favor of his "sacred herb"—absinthe—he adored it for fishing and canoeing. The Seine offered countless happy hours which Jarry shared with his friends at the Phalanstère. It is said that his noteworthy skill as a fisherman sustained him when he lacked money for food.

Jarry's financial state was grim despite his continued productivity. Before the turn of the century, he published his most esoteric work, *L'Amour absolu* [Absolute Love], a son's pathological tribute to his mother. In a completely different vein, he published the *Almanach du Père Ubu,* illustrated by Pierre Bonnard, in which one finds many ubuesque comments on contemporary life in the capital and predictions of such events as a partial eclipse of Père Ubu from 29 to 30 February 1899. By the fall of 1899, Jarry had also completed *Ubu Enchaîné* [Ubu Enchained]. That same year the *Mercure de France* published a companion piece to *Faustroll* (which would not be published until 1911) entitled "Commentaire pour servir à la construction pratique de la machine à explorer le temps" [Commentary to Help in the Practical Construction of the Time-Machine]. In it, Jarry presents the practical and theoretical considerations of exploring time, making use of

Henri Bergson's recent teachings on distinguishing time from duration. The speculations mimic those of H. G. Wells's *The Time Machine,* just translated into French that year.[17]

Self-destruction: 1900–1907

It was 1900 and Jarry was twenty-seven years old. Père Ubu's extravagant mask had conclusively replaced the pallid face that could once be glimpsed beneath it. Along with his health, the vigor of his writing began to wane. After 1900, he managed only one magisterial work, his "modern novel," *The Supermale,* published in 1902 by the *Revue blanche.* Aside from that, he turned out a twentieth-century *Almanach du Père Ubu,* a rather bizarre "novel of Ancient Rome" entitled *Messaline,* and a romping translation of Christian Grabbe's *Scherz, Satire, Ironie und tiefere Bedeutung* under the name of *Les Silènes.* He published a reworked *Par la taille,* a shortened marionette version of *King Ubu* called *Ubu sur la butte* [Ubu on the Montmartre Hill], and an uninspired operetta, *Le Moutardier du pape,*[18] which sold only owing to the efforts of friends to provide him with some income. His contributions to various periodicals continued, and thanks to "Gestes" [Exploits], his regular humorous articles in the *Revue blanche,* he subsisted in a stable enough economic situation for three years, until the review folded in 1903. Jarry dedicated *The Supermale* to its coowner Thadée Natanson. It was not until 1969 that a collection of Jarry's articles was published under the rubric *La Chandelle verte* [The Green Candle], in honor of the favored invocation of Père Ubu: "de par ma chandelle verte." The articles, compiled and presented by Maurice Saillet, include the "Speculations" and "Exploits" which appeared in the *Revue blanche,* as well as Jarry's contributions to reviews such as *Le Canard Sauvage, L'Oeil, Poesia,* and *La Plume.* The compilation reveals the incredible variety of topics familiar to Jarry: he covered diverse trades, science, sports, inventions, fashion, art, and literature.

Jarry stubbornly refused to accept material assistance from his friends. Despite offers of help, he did without food on more than a few occasions, once he could no longer depend on a salary from the now-defunct *Revue blanche.* His flirtation with the *Figaro* ended when he balked at the notion of a newspaper deadline. Notoriously addicted to individual liberty, as well as to ether, which became his major vice—it was cheaper than absinthe— Jarry determinedly stalked absolute freedom, even though it led him to self-destruction.

He seemed pulled in two directions: on the one hand, he never abandoned writing. In the mountains at Dauphiné, from November 1903 to May 1904, he worked on a libretto of *Pantagruel* (with music by Claude Terrasse), consulting former versions of the work at the library in Lyon. On the other hand, his deteriorating state precluded any serious creativity. During the winter of 1905–6, the destitute Jarry could not heat the Chasublerie; he socialized less and less. Before his death the following year, he nonetheless undertook two further projects. With Dr. Saltas, he began a translation from modern Greek of Emmanuel Rhoides's *La Papesse Jeanne* [Pope Jean]. Saltas agreed without hesitation to Jarry's proposal of collaboration—insisting that they work at his home—in order to care for his friend without offending Père Ubu's inflated pride. Jarry's rapidly failing health soon necessitated a visit to Laval, where he could rest under his sister's supervision. Through moments of lucidity interspersed with bouts of fever and utter fatigue, he worked on his last novel, *La Dragonne*. Pages of the manuscript are illegible. He never completed it, but while in Laval he dictated to Charlotte plans for the complete work.[19]

Against all odds, having already received the last rites, he recuperated sufficiently to return to Paris in the spring of 1907, where he would die after several return visits to Laval following relapses that became more and more threatening. He maintained the Chasublerie and journeyed back to his legendary apartment for the final time thanks to the generosity of the Natanson brothers. Shortly after his return, he was found on the floor, semiconscious, his legs paralyzed. Vallette and Saltas had him taken immediately to the hospital, where his case was pronounced hopeless. In spite of his relatively cheerful front and attempts at "normalcy," few of his friends had the stomach for more than one visit. At the age of thirty-four, Jarry could physically no longer sustain the savage pose he had chosen to assume. His motor gave out, as he predicted it would in a letter to Rachilde. In that same letter, written from Laval on 28 May 1906, he asserted once again his unfailing belief in the liberating power of the human imagination: "He [Père Ubu] believes that the brain, during decomposition, continues to function after death, and that its dreams are our Paradise."[20]

He probably would have been pleased by the turnout at his funeral: the Vallettes were there, along with such notables as Paul Léautaud, Octave Mirbeau, Félix Fénéon, Pierre Bonnard, Léon-Paul Fargue, and Paul Valéry, among others. The scene after the service at the cemetery of Bagneux was not morose. The mourners knew Père Ubu would appreciate levity and the clinking of glasses.

Chapter Two
Pataphysically Speaking . . .

What lent Jarry's brief life its coherence was his work. Forays into his text reveal a fundamental continuity resulting from his theory of Pataphysics. The text focalizes and concretely organizes Jarry's indestructible yearnings to escape the routine and the commonplace. Pataphysics serves as the locus of both oneiric and rhetorical displacement. It provides access to another dimension of thought and of language.

Pataphysics permeates the warp and the woof of Jarry's creation, and its inventor underscores its significance formulaically in many telling passages. By granting privilege to this pseudoscience Jarry acceded to a particular hyperbolic version of life and literature. Like a mirror in a funhouse, his writings present a most unexpected portrayal of reality, at once a deformation and an exaggeration. Calculated tampering with "reality" triggers catastrophic or providential changes; the imaginary hypothesis replaces the known or the probable and insinuates itself into the order of things as reality. The texts' constantly shifting perspectives establish the possible, rather than the probable, as credible.

Collecting the Data

Pataphysics first appeared in Jarry's works as a means of identifying Ubu:[1] his calling card announces him as a *docteur en pataphysique*. "Pataphysics," Ubu explains to his baffled host, "is a science that we [Ubu always uses the royal "we"] invented and for which the need was generally felt" (*Les Minutes de sable mémorial,* 182). In another section of "Puppet Show," Ubu calls

Pataphysics "our Science," stressing its superiority over ordinary science (small "s"). Obviously preoccupied with an elaboration of this science of sciences, in 1894 Jarry stated (in a note preceding *Les Minutes de sable mémorial*) that he was preparing "Elements of Pataphysics," which ultimately became Book II of *Exploits and Opinions of Doctor Faustroll, Pataphysician.* This philosophicoscientific system known as Pataphysics motivated Jarry's earliest literary endeavors. His writings, often deemed chaotic and obscure, constitute a subtle composition of dexterously executed reformulations and reapplications of pataphysical axioms.

Ineluctably, Pataphysics extended its purview throughout Jarry's career. Less tendentious than personal, however, his works remained highly hermetic, often dense precisely because of their pataphysical frameworks. For, as Jarry cannily teaches, "simplicity need not be simple, but condensed and synthesized complexity" ("Linteau," 172). His heraldic play *César-Antechrist* offers a virtuoso performance of this basic pataphysical fact. One person contains all contradictions within himself. Here, the Christ and the Antichrist are but alternating forms of the same Being who synthesizes all opposites. Cognizant himself of the daunting nature of Pataphysics, Jarry periodically inserted explicit, if not easily accessible, references to his science. In *Days and Nights,* amid vatic chants and mesmerizing visions, Jarry included a chapter entitled "Pataphysique" devoted to a demonstration of how one lives pataphysically: thoughts, volition, and acts become as indistinguishable as the days and nights of the title. This chapter illustrates the interdependence and the equivalence of everything. By virtue of willpower, thought can be directly transformed into action in the world surrounding the individual. The spiritual and the material realms are not only inseparable but commingle.

Despite the vicissitudes of daily existence, Jarry steadfastly chose fidelity to the pataphysical universe. Fanciful, ironic, or mystical, his writing never lacked the deliberate combination of verve, mockery, and utmost seriousness characteristic of Pataphysics. Its provenance, perhaps, supplies the reason: it was in Monsieur Félix Hébert's physics class that the seed was sown.

But Pataphysics, it has been argued, is as ancient as thought itself, having existed

ever since a man first scratched his head to quell the itch of reflective thought, ever since Socrates demonstrated to Meno that his slave boy had known the Pythagorean theorem all along, ever since the day Panurge defeated the English scholar in a disputation by signs, ever since Lewis Carroll established the equivalence of cabbages and kings.[2]

Nevertheless Pataphysics awaited the agile mind of Alfred Jarry for its quintessential formulation. While the ill-fated teacher persevered with pompous phraseology and botched experiments, and while the legend that was to culminate in the creation of Ubu devolved to a new generation of schoolboys, Jarry learned that science was a rigorous method whereby one could imagine, and consequently create, a World. Forever indebted to the misguided teachings of the physics professor, Jarry would structure his fiction with terminology, information, and intuitions culled from so-called real science, but would inform his work with the combined zaniness and gravity of a chemical reaction gone berserk.

Faustroll: The Formula

Exploits and Opinions of Doctor Faustroll, Pataphysician is not at all a traditional novel. Composed of eight books, each divided into from two to fourteen chapters, it links various episodes, in which the Doctor and his crew appear, to philosophical reflections and scientific nonsense. Our introduction to Faustroll places him in a difficult situation. Served with a notice to pay his rent he triumphs over adversity, deciding to embark on a fabulous voyage in a boat made from a sieve. The second book first defines "Pataphysics," then describes a bizarre experience in which Faustroll is transported to the pataphysical universe, much like Alice, who shrinks conveniently in Wonderland. Finally, a chapter introduces in some detail Faustroll's chief mate, a stupid baboon, named Bosse-de-Nage because of his callused, enlarged derrière. The third and longest book recounts the strange voyage, devoting a chapter to each island visited. The next four books are a conglomeration of incidents and delirious speculations. The last book, "Ethernity," places Faustroll in the afterlife, where he does his utmost—as a trusty scientist—to orient himself and "survive" his own death. The novel's penultimate statement scientifically defines "God's surface."

Summing up, a concluding emphatic statement, *"Pataphysics is the science . . . ,"* leaves the reader in suspense, displacing attention and desire into a hypothetical, imaginary future and an unknown blank space. The reader finishes by taking over the helm for Faustroll, caught in the game of presence and absence, in the structure of infinite quest and rebirth which underpins most of Jarry's dramatic and narrative works.

Jarry's Rabelaisian novel most completely details the tenets of his invented science.[3] It champions the individual's perception and the exception rather than the general rule, unlike conventional science. Pataphysics, since it operates according to individual volition, differs from any conceptual science: Jarry sought a thought system that could function both as an inner attitude and as a lived experience. He reserves a chapter of *Faustroll* for its formal definition: "Pataphysics is the science of imaginary solutions, that symbolically attributes the properties of objects, described by their virtuality, to lineaments." Witness Jarry's classic example of objects described according to their "virtual lineaments":

Why does everyone affirm that the shape of a watch is round, which is manifestly false, since in profile it looks like a narrow rectangle, elliptical from a three-quarter view, and why the devil have people only taken note of its shape at the moment they look at the time? (*Faustroll*, 669)

Pataphysics describes the "supplementary universe," exposing the accidental or the unexpected in an apparently ordinary or predictable situation.

The science of the Possible, not the Probable, Pataphysics studies the aberrant and the absurd. Jarry dubs the temporal medium of this imaginary domain "ethernity," combining his precious ether (which permits his escape from the banal world of clocks and standards) with eternity (the continuous dimension of the absolute). Exploring ethernity, Faustroll—along with Jarry's other characters, and, indeed, Jarry himself—remains unconcerned with religion, morality, beauty, or change of any kind. Value systems are simply beside the point in the universe that Jarry devised to replace the traditional one. In a typical pataphysical "proof," Faustroll logically concludes that God, being the shortest path from zero to infinity, is the point tangential to both (731).

Such lucubrations are made possible by Pataphysics's two most consequential principles: first, the universal equivalence of all things; second, the periodic conversion of opposites between poles. The identity and reconciliation of opposites (for example, being/living, zero/infinity, plus/minus, day/night), in conjunction with the rejection of any hierarchy of values, open the door to a universe where life is perceived as irrational, absurd, at times hallucinatory, and always ludicrous. These precepts grant entry to a world similar to the dream, the masked ritual, the narcotic or psychotic hallucination. This realm condenses immense networks of information and images, schematizing them into symbolic representations and processes. Cryptic and transformational in the same sense as is a mathematical equation, Pataphysics alchemizes the ordinary (water, for example, must be revitalized so that it becomes extraordinary) while simultaneously unmasking the illusory nature of objectivity which traditional science purports to respect.

In accordance with pataphysical laws, which dismantle standards of perception generally presumed adequate to measure and represent reality, Doctor Faustroll, miniaturized to the size of a mite, strolls along a cabbage leaf. His scrutiny of the transparent elastic spheres positioned on the leaf reveals them to be water droplets. From his new vantage point, they are twice his size and seem to be gigantic crystal globes. The imperturbable pataphysician interprets the world exclusively as a function of his perception.

Faustroll: The Demonstration

A dashing captain, clean-shaven but for his sea-green moustache, his gold-tone complexion contrasting handsomely with his hair—alternating hair by hair ash blond and darkest black—Faustroll wears a shirt of woven quartz fiber. His skiff is constructed of the same material, a resistant suspension wire developed by the British scientist Charles Vernon Boys.[4] Faustroll's floating sieve depends on the laws of surface tension, weightless membranes, surfaces of no curvature, and the elastic skin of water, all phenomena central to Boys's experiments. The vessel itself, a formal testimony to the validity of paradox, represents an emblem of Jarry's intellectual system and his process of creation. It is another instance of the text reaching out its tentacles to entrap and assimilate a morsel of reality, so that the imaginary cannot be distinguished from the real.

A good deal of the Faustrollian universe recasts diverse scientific documents into literature. Pataphysics equates and merges life and art, equal and/because opposite. Fancy often embellishes fact and presumed fantasy often merely transposes segments of reality. It is less mystifying, in this context, to learn that the odyssey to exotic shores takes place not on water, that suspect standard of density and bacteria-ridden liquid, but on Jarry's beloved Parisian sidewalks. Faustroll shows his pataphysical mettle by sailing from Paris to Paris in a sieve, a trip all the more incredible because it is narrated by the bailiff who delivered the summons to pay the rent. Thus, even the (fictional) representative of bureaucratic reality becomes a party to the fantastic adventure. There is no "off-stage."

Doctor Faustroll incessantly deforms "objective" reality, nullifying reason by means of intellectual tools (such as logical deduction) and through the use of paradox, a key element of pataphysical reasoning. Conflict between the microcosmic world of the individual and the macrocosm external to him cedes to "imaginary solutions." Time dissolves: an eternal present disguised as infinite space invades consciousness. Thus, Faustroll and his entourage travel not through the dimension of time in order to explore memories, but through a spatial continuum. It is a recognition of the power of language over reality to create a spatial representation of what is logically outside the dimension of space. Faustroll's itinerary has more to do with the landscape of memory and imagination than with tangible geography.

Indeed, the memories explored by Faustroll—geographical realities on the map of the "supplementary universe"—are explicit spatial translations of *texts* (and, to a lesser degree, codes of music, drawing, and painting) read (heard, seen) by Jarry. Paradoxically, Jarry intimates that Faustroll owes his exploration of the unknown to the body of knowledge constituted by these works. Like his namesake, the legendary Faust, Doctor Faustroll incarnates the will to absolute knowledge, complementing the instinctual Ubu: Jarry was a visionary always in intimate contact with the earthy. Faustroll's reality is none other than an imaginative recasting of the artistic and scientific imagination of others (such as the British scientists Lord Kelvin and C. V. Boys, the writers Franc-Nohain and Mallarmé, the artists Gauguin and Beardsley, and the composer Claude Terrasse).

As he displaces reality by exploring thought rendered spatial, Faustroll fulfills Jarry's indomitable scopic drive: to see, to act, to know. He and his crew navigate on *terra firma,* visiting so-called islands, each of which spatializes features Jarry judged pertinent in a given work of art he experienced. But paradoxically, this spatial reality is undermined by the very fact that it exists solely on a linguistic plane, that is, in yet another text. By abstracting and giving spatial presence to certain qualities of a chosen work, in a sense Jarry created a *mask* of that work. Faustroll, then, becomes a spectator of the mask (and psychic drama) constituted by each island. Jarry created a witness to his own *thought in action.*

The relationship between the work of another creator selected by Jarry and the literary mask of that work in *Faustroll* is curiously theatrical. Jarry abstracted what he considered the salient characteristics of another's creation and made them visually concrete in terms of a descriptive décor strategically distanced from the existing work that served as a point of departure for Jarry's own fiction. Faustroll operates inside this mask-turned-décor, and by virtue of observing it, attributes reality to the imaginary, condensed and structured by a spatial form. This anomalous reflexivity thus adapts theatrical modes of production to the novelistic genre. And just as Jarry places Faustroll—who gives form to a crucial aspect of Jarry's personality—before the spectacle of his own mind, Faustroll finds himself observed, in turn, within the textual universe, by his companion Bosse-de-Nage. Jarry honed the stratification of dramatic distancing and doubling to perfection. These structures of displacement and mirroring typify his fictional writing.

One of the dozen islands to which Faustroll sails in his floating sieve—and which exemplifies Jarry's literary tactics—is l'Ile Amorphe ("The Amorphic Island"). The chapter recounting this adventure transposes *Petits poèmes amorphes* [Short Amorphic Poems] by Franc-Nohain, to whom Jarry dedicated the chapter. (Each chapter is dedicated to the artist whose work is represented in it.) On the one hand, this chapter functions as an evocation of the literary world created by Franc-Nohain; on the other hand, it specifies certain components of that world as germane to Jarry's aesthetics. Thus, *Faustroll* contains a metasemiotic text that ingeniously comments at once on the works of Jarry's contemporaries and on his own. The text reveals its own inner workings and glosses its own production.

Naturally, the principal attribute of the island reminiscent of *Petits poèmes amorphes* is its formlessness, "comparable to soft, amoebic and protoplasmic coral" (681). Jarry parodies Franc-Nohain's excessive attention to the meanings and uses of the term "amorphic" by transposing it to an incongruous physical setting, that is, by transferring the rhetorical plane of *Petits poèmes amorphes* to the literal one of the "Amorphic Island." Jarry's description of the island continues: "its trees differed little from the gesture of the snail. . . ." Jarry converts this evidently spiraled protoplasm into the beguiling metaphor of the brain. Faustroll, it follows, journeys through this cerebral matter (Jarry's?) replete with pataphysical symbols.

The oligarchic government of the island is emblematic of Jarry's splintered personality. Ruled by six kings, each of whom elucidates a facet of Jarry's psyche, the island/brain serves as a compelling model for Jarry's opus. It is not surprising that just prior to his death, Jarry confided to his friend Rachilde his belief that, after death, the decomposing brain's dreams are paradisaical. The absolute is attainable only through the fecund destruction offered by death.

A banquet on this island paradise occasions Faustroll's description of its kings. The first sports a "psychent" (a double crown symbolizing the pharaoh's sovereignty over Lower and Upper Egypt) signifying, in Jarry's iconography, his duplex nature, especially the doubling of the head, wherein resides the all-important brain. He personifies Jarry's quest for the absolute in three ways: first, by escaping the law (in this case his Parliament), like Faustroll, who undertakes his voyage to avoid legal action for not paying his rent, and like Sengle, who deserts the army in *Days and Nights.* The second clue that he represents the desire for the absolute is the fact that he "works, sleeps, loves, and drinks on the vertical axis of a large ladder" (681), verticality symbolizing the aspiration for the absolute. The ladder itself is symbolic of the passage from one mode of existence to another and signifies the imaginary voyage of escape to a "hyper, or supra, celestial place."[5] A third indication of the pure realm of the absolute is the king's explicit resemblance to Saint Siméon Stylites.

During his escape from justice, the king takes refuge in a monolith set in the main square. The vertical column's obvious phallic connotation links two concepts central to Jarry's work: sexuality and purity, concepts expertly developed in *The Supermale.* Throughout, the realms of the terrestrial and the celestial exist in counterpoint, exemplified by Ubu, the instinctual; and Faustroll, the intellectual. To attempt a merger of the two represents, in Jarry's works, a lethal drive.

In addition to his already multiple symbolism, the first king, like Jarry, makes of debauchery a habit that provides his only "illumination." The amusing icing on the cake is the king's final accomplishment: he invented "the tandem, which extends the advantage of the pedal to quadrupeds" (681). Pataphysical at all costs, Jarry never failed to poke fun at his own eccentricity.

Jarry fashioned the second king, too, in his own image. In this case, two obsessions—fishing and locomotives—enter into mortal conflict. In a nightmarish superimposition of images of river beds and railroad tracks, based on their structural identity, trains "pursue the fish in front of them or crush, in their belly, the embryos of bites" (682). This elliptical passage emphasizes sadism, manifest in the symbolism of biting which appears in many of Jarry's works, and dangerous—indeed deadly—internal space.[6] The railroad tracks—in an unconventional and provocative image—blossom surrealistically from the king's fishing rod. The sadistic aggressivity is a blatant extension of the king himself and represents a projection of an omnipotent, bestial Self.

The third king embodies Jarry's need for perfection. Poet, scientist, and mathematician, this king has "rediscovered paradisaical language, intelligible even to animals," as well as having "manufactured electric dragon-flies and enumerated the innumerable ants with the figure of the numeral 3" (682). Jarry limns a portrait—albeit a ludicrous one—of the ultimate pundit: the inspired yet rational man.

By means of the fourth king, Jarry derides the members of the French Academy, an institution responsible for maintaining standards of the French language. This king's instruction would reform Faustroll. The latter would renounce drink—perhaps the only *un*imaginable possibility in this bizarre "story"—and, putting his time to good use, would be recognized by the Academy. Indeed, Book III ("From Paris to Paris by Sea or the Belgian Robinson") begins with a quotation from Rabelais's *Gargantua* on the subject of wine: a people may be judged by the wine they drink. Alcohol, not surprisingly, symbolizes the union of active and passive principles in a fluid, shifting relationship at once creative and destructive.

The fact that the king in question is noticeably clean-shaven, however, begs comparison with the Supermale's split persona. Like the king, the Supermale presents a facade of civility and respectability symbolized here by the Academy. It is only when the Supermale assumes his role of the instinctual, aggressive Indian that his clean-shavenness is mentioned. Ostensibly reputable, the king, too, Jarry suggests, must be concealing those drives society teaches us to repress. It is not accidental that Jarry's own textual doubles reproduce his intrapsychic multiplicities.

Jarry's fecund psyche engendered a marionettist as the fifth king. Theater of the marionette impassioned Jarry primarily because it obviated the need to transmit ideas through the vehicle of another human being. As the king explains, he chose puppets "so that there be nothing in [the characters] but purity" (682). As early as his *lycée* days, Jarry enjoyed writing for and staging puppet theater which avoids human specificity.

The sixth, and final, king represents not an aspect of Jarry's personality per se, but Franc-Nohain himself, whom Jarry chose to honor in *Faustroll*. In a literary game where "reality" is constantly in question, Jarry fabricated a symbolic Franc-Nohain who functions as a character in a setting that reproduces, in a spatial context, his own text. But since it is precisely the abstraction of *Petits poèmes amorphes* accomplished by Jarry that serves as the setting, the writer-king is, ultimately, an avatar of Jarry's protean fictional Self.

The complexity of this two-page densely packed, illustrative chapter does not stop here. Faustroll's own Double, Bosse-de-Nage, becomes a spectator of the banquet attended by Faustroll and the kings, having been assigned the task of holding the foot of the ladder upon which the festivities occur. The ladder thus serves as a vertical stage. Faustroll witnesses *and* participates in an enactment of Jarry's self-transformations, distanced spatially within the textual décor, the whole taking place in the framework of a spatial rendering of Franc-Nohain's book.

Faustroll, by scoffing at the forces of "Law and Justice" and setting sail, acquits himself of time as duration and ventures into the supplementary universe. He travels through the spatial medium of "ethernity" which permits creative consciousness to be materialized and acted out. Such a hyperbolic world exists only virtually. He who enters it experiences an initiation rite in which Jarry appropriates and parodies the creative fantasy of others, transforming it into his personal literary mask. Each island encountered during the voyage is the site of a spectacle thanks to which Jarry exteriorizes the anguish and the laughter of his divided self. Doctor Faustroll's adventures demonstrate how Pataphysics set in motion—Jarry's existential and literary mask—accomplishes a fortuitous sublimation of dangerous drives, constructing an Absolute out of a shattered psyche.

Inspired on the one hand by Goethe's *Faust* (especially Part II), Jarry created his own rebel, an incarnation of man's quest to penetrate the paradoxes of life and his thirst for ultimate knowledge. On the other hand, Jarry incorporated the character of the troll into his own antihero. He himself acted the role of King of the Trolls in Ibsen's *Peer Gynt* at the *Theatre de l'Oeuvre*. Trolls, gnomelike malicious demons of Scandinavian folklore, personify the "dark" forces of nature (or the unconscious) and physically resemble the Homunculus alchemically fabricated in Goethe's work, as well as resembling Bosse-de-Nage, Doctor Faustroll's loyal servant. Faust and the troll, the intellect and the id, combine to produce Faustroll, who, like his component namesakes, is an avatar of what psychologist Carl Jung termed the "motif of the child archetype." Jung cites *Faust* as a key example of this archetypal motif.

Transformational energy and the concept of rebirth characterize the child archetype. It is not a question of any traditional figure of the child, but of a mystical and spontaneous vision: the unforeseen rebirth of a lost savior. This transformation does not imply redemption in a moral or religious sense: the mode is purely mythical and symbolic. Naturally, the rebirth occurs in an improbable fashion and the so-called savior assumes a perfect and divine form. Such is, in fact, the bizarre birth of Faustroll, born at the age of sixty-three, when the "twentieth century was (-2) years old" (658), the same age at which he "dies." Moreover, he proclaims his own divinity. He responds for his shipmates to the query, "Are you Christians?" by the categorical affirmation, "I am God" (679).

Divine, born and raised in extraordinary circumstances, the child-god is not a human child. Therefore, according to Jung, he materializes by means of the most diverse forms: god, giant, animal, Tom Thumb. Apropos is a miniaturized Faustroll strolling on a cabbage leaf in a chapter significantly entitled "Faustroll Smaller than Faustroll." Jung described the child as an evolution toward a state of lucidity of the Self and specified, referring to the Self, that as an individual phenomenon he is "smaller than small," while as an equivalent of the cosmos, he is "bigger than big."[7]

If Faustroll's life is exceptional, his supposed death is even more unique. Having expired at the same age at which he was born, he telepathically communicates with the earth-bound scientist Lord Kelvin: "Death is only for mediocre people. Nevertheless it is true that I am no longer on earth. [. . .] I was in that locale where one is when one has left time and space, infinite eternity, Sir" (724–25).

During Faustroll's visit to the island/music of Claude Terrasse (who collaborated on the music of *King Ubu*'s premiere), just after a farewell toast, a song arises. "On two pillars raised toward two heavenly bodies that struck the hours of union and division of the black key and the diurnal key, a small naked child and a white-haired old man were singing toward the double disk of silver and gold" (692). The song is a rendition of the words "Let's drink night and day, let love always occupy us." But Jarry's linguistic contorsions make the verse obscene thus unifying—pataphysically—the purest and the rankest utterance, become simultaneously spiritual (Faust) and earthly (troll).

During his performance, the "white-bearded energumen" gestures wildly. By means of an obscene and puerile language that recalls Ubu's, he exteriorizes a deadly anguish: the two faces of the theatricalization of the Self. From aboard their craft, Faustroll and clan observe the ravings of the old man. From his vantage point Faustroll witnesses the old man's mask falling off, the tangible drama of his own psyche exteriorized before his eyes. Behind this possessed wizard hides a middle-aged dwarf with a sordid beard. He is, after all, the incarnation of the mystical child described by Jung, that part of Faustroll himself who resembles the troll of *Peer Gynt* but at the same time that part of him which

imitates the white-bearded sage. Faustroll thus becomes the spectator of his own drama, of his own disquieting mascarade, witness
to the dramatic schism of his own personality.

Caesar-Antichrist: The Experiment

Classical character development did not interest Jarry. A master
of atmosphere and suggestion, he preferred depicting man's self-
exploration. This four-act heraldic play proved the perfect forum
for his talents and proclivities. In this intricate and crepuscular
play, the inward journey reveals the equality of all things: within
himself, man discovers both the Christ and the Antichrist. With
considerable economy, using a highly complex network of images,
Jarry portrays a universe in which neither form nor substance
poses an obstacle to transformation. The animate and the inanimate, life and death, plus and minus, not only coexist equally
in one being, but one generates the other and vice versa. Generative force suffices to swing the pendulum toward one or the
other incarnation of the Self. Essentially, man divines that he is
suspended between poles, like the zero that reconciles opposites.
Jarry makes frequent use of the specular image to elucidate the
inversion and the conversion of one world into the other.

Caesar-Antichrist's changes are represented by a series of heraldic emblems. The penchant for graphic expression exhibited
by Jarry in *l'Ymagier* accounts here too for his use of pure visual
signification. As the characters progress from Act to Act, from
realm to realm, their transformations abide by Jarry's interpretation of the temporal and the spatial. These quasi-ritualistic,
imagistic processes poetically confuse the worlds of the Christ
and the Antichrist. It is through the world of the Self, we are
led to conclude, that all other worlds exist and submit to our
penetration. Mutations and transformations of time, space, matter, and language break the sociocultural carapace that traditionally limits the subject. *Caesar-Antichrist* is a tour de force of
theater of the mind; it recuperates the unmediated vision of a
self which denies distinctions between realms of being. The expanded, heightened consciousness of the pataphysician renews the
bonds with what is repressed within him, and, in so doing,

neutralizes the specific opposition of such poles as negative and positive, zero and infinity, diastole and systole, desire and prohibition, savage and civilized. Jarry's deft use of occult symbolism renders problematical the very framework of opposition. In *Faustroll*, Ibicratus the Geometer (in a dialogue parodying those of Plato) expounds,

The juxtaposition of the two signs, of the binary and the ternary, gives the figure of the letter H, which is Chronos, father of Time or of Life, and thus includes men. For the Geometer, these two signs annul or fecundate one another, and only their fruit subsists, which becomes the egg or the zero, all the more identical, since they are opposites. And from the dispute of the Plus sign and the Minus sign, the Reverend Father Ubu, of the Company of Jesus, former king of Poland, wrote a book whose title is *Caesar-Antichrist,* where one finds the only practical demonstration, by the mechanical engine called *bâton-à-physique,* of the identity of opposites. (730)

Caesar-Antichrist, addressing the three Christs as one, explains, "I am the sovereign mirror that reflects you: you penetrate me and that is why I am your opposite. And with my perverse shrewdness I say to you, holding you enclosed in me: it is you who are my opposite and reflect me. . . . Man is the line of collapse between the two of us, the null plane where two twin soap bubbles embrace" (281). Each pole is at once itself and its contrary; each pole, "being" its opposite, reappears endlessly in it. No pole, for Jarry, exists independently. Rather, it is a question of eternal flux, of intermediaries, of a dynamic process obliged to repeat itself. Man remains suspended between the infinite positive principle and its inverse. "Men," writes Jarry, " are the Middle, between Infinity and Nothingness, pulled painfully by the arcs of a zero" (290). Oneness in duality is similarly exhibited by Bosse-de-Nage, in *Faustroll,* whose customary utterance is the "succinct" expression "Ha Ha!" Pronounced in French, "A A," the articulation of this echoed sound ("A juxtaposed to A") formulates the identity principle while simultaneously deconstructing it. "The two A's differ in space, when we write them, if not time, in the same way that two twins are not born together [. . .]. Pronounced quickly enough, to the point of merging, this is the idea of unity. Slowly, of duality, of the echo, of distance, of symmetry, of greatness, and of duration, the two principles of good and evil" (704).

Jarry's subversion of discourse—by means of substituting for words visual ciphers such as a letter of the alphabet or by means of evoking symbols of infinity and nullity—corresponds to his desire to convert his scribal gesture into a theatrical one. He suggests that another universe exists which surpasses even the absurd and the paradoxical, and that such a universe might be coherent if one were to make the leap into a new dimension. Like the Cabalists, Jarry posited words—no longer purely conceptual—possessing creative powers. That is why, undermining his sham construction of verbal opposites, Jarry's imagery understandably symbolizes circularity and unity: the sphere, the hermaphrodite, the rotating *bâton-à-physique* (a magic wand which generates a circle from a spinning minus sign via the intermediary plus sign achieved by a one-quarter turn), the Trinity, the nyctalopic (i.e., dayblind) pupil, the crown (of gold and of thorns).

The Christ and the Antichrist are thus one Being passing through two (opposing and reversible) stages of existence. The mainspring of the play's structure depends on the cyclic nature of the alternation between poles. Each of the four acts represents a temporal progression in the life of this multiple Being. Time and space are conflated so that the changes in time become discontinuous, spatial displacements. Whence the heraldic décor, schematic and complex—Jarry's "condensed simplicity"—which serves as a compact graphic emblem of his entire opus. When, at the end of the second act, the terrestrial form of the Antichrist germinates, it is none other than Ubu who asks, "Who will be King?" Three escutcheons reply by arranging themselves in the proper order to spell, by their respective shapes, "T.O.Y.," Old French for "you." The following act ("The Terrestrial Act"), depicting the earthly sojourn of the Antichrist, is a prototext of the Ubu Cycle, entitled "King Ubu."

In the final act, Ubu, ascended and newly transformed into Caesar, reflects on his experiences, accompanied by the Sphinx,

symbol of mythic femininity, and yet another model of the union
of opposites. As Caesar-Antichrist, he meditates,

> I slept, my soul slept, my active body crept about, my Double. When
> one sees one's double, one dies. . . . I want to rise out of this ground
> that will be mobile and trembling and will revolt beneath me when
> the Other comes to live his terrestrial dream. . . . (327)

Doubling is the thematic and structural grid of Jarry's play. Here
and elsewhere, throughout his literary corpus, beneath the retinue
of attendant mathematical, theological, and other symbols of the
Double, an infratext performs a sacralization of a masculine and
phallocentric sexuality.

The protean metaphor of the phallus finds its most adequate
representation in the *Bâton-à-physique,* a stick or staff, whose
equivalence—on various levels of manifest and connotative content—to Christ, to the Antichrist, and to Ubu is established.[8]
In the second act, "The Heraldic Act," the *Bâton-à-physique* appears as a character and is addressed by the Templar: "Uprooted
Phallus, do not jump about like that!" (289). This alludes overtly
to a sexually charged passage in Lautréamont's *Les Chants de
Maldoror* in which God leaves an uprooted hair in a brothel.
Moreover, the movement of the baton visually proves its divinity:
in a horizontal position it designates a minus sign; when it turns
perpendicularly around its median point it becomes a plus sign.
Thus, this shifting, spinning signifier reconciles opposites by its
own unstable form. It is at once, according to characters wit-
nessing its acrobatics, a line and a circle, negative and positive,
man and woman, sex and spirit. In a veritable verbal orgy, this
slippery baton is endowed with a plurality of meaning: a wheel
retaining only its diameter, an eye, half Holy Spirit, somersault-
ing skeleton, Christ, Saint Peter, the owl, the Cross, the emblem
of spontaneous generation, polyhedral infinity, the dagger, flam-
ing impalement post, a globe equal to the earth, a hermaphrodite
(289–90). Like the baton, the hermaphrodite represents the union
of the most polar opposites in an intense figure harking back to
a primitive state of consciousness which did not formalize contrasts. In addition, it is specified as the ideal form of the child-

god archetype. In "The Terrestrial Act" the *bâton-à-physique* is one of Ubu's most important weapons. Because of its attributes elsewhere in the play, its connotation in this farcical act is greatly extended.

Why did Jarry include the exploits of Ubu as the "Terrestrial Act" of *Caesar-Antichrist?* Why put the story of the burlesque, grotesque schoolboy creation on the same footing as a work as poetically sumptuous, as esoteric, and as erudite as this? Behind the curious incongruence of the two registers of writing lurks the pataphysical conception of opposites, materialized by the *bâton-à-physique*. Jarry thus transposes his theory into the very workings of his text which literally gives form, on the level of semiological signs (as compared to the mathematical signs of the manifest content), to the "science of imaginary solutions." Pataphysics governs the content *and* the form of the play, whose reading is consonant with Jarry's entire creation. The dispute between the Plus and the Minus signs incorporated in the *bâton-à-physique* and rendered null by both the point and the zero, duplicates the relationship between the universe of Caesar or of Christ and that of Ubu. The former is that of the positive sign, the latter the negative (or non −) sign. The existence of the "Terrestrial Act" in the midst of *Caesar-Antichrist* deconstructs both of them by the fact of their purported equivalence. Self-de(con)struction on a textual as well as existential plane, seems to be the suicidal apotheosis which results, in Jarry's case, from a horrendous excess of self-permutations.

It is never easy to determine the relationship between the signs in *Caesar-Antichrist* and their referents. Every image, in this labyrinth of images, can refer to several referents, each one appropriate at a different point of the play. Caesar-Antichrist (in Acts II and IV) is himself only another form of the golden cross (Act I) and Ubu (Act III). The Christian world is presented as its mirror-image. Reversals and inversions both structure the play and account for the many references to inverted beings. Near the end of the play, God the Father in fact takes a mirror-image to be his true son. Language also participates in the game of reversal: in the first act, Saint Peter says to the golden Christ, "I thrice denied God, and by my denial, faith tripled, I created that upside-down trinity whose loving arms suffocate me" (274). Indeed, the Antichrist's omniscience claims its source in experiencing the simultaneous existence of two polar infinities. Man, finally, is the point where the negative meets the positive magnitude, at once the line where "two twin soap bubbles embrace" (281) and the point between the "two arcs of zero" which form the infinity sign, between "Infinity and Nothingness" (281), the plane mirror separating reality from its reflected image.

Etre et Vivre: The Corollary

Etre et Vivre [To Be and To Live], a short text related to Caesar-Antichrist, is introduced by an excerpt from a dialogue in which Ubu declares himself to be a great pataphysician and inventor of the much-needed science of Pataphysics. In the short, philosophical essay, To Be and To Live, a twenty-year-old Jarry strikes the pose of a staunch supporter of Being, only to lead his reader astray, and finish on the side of its opposite, that is, Living. He goes so far as to advise the "murder" of being. Death functions as a mediator between Being and Living:[9] death, the absolute reconciliation between opposites, arrests the dialectic and offers a tantalizing liberation from the terrorism of psychic mobility.

The opposition of Being to Living pits Eternity, Idea, Continuum, and Infinite Space against Duration, Action, Discontinuum, and Enclosure. Living means having an organic connection to the flow of time, which, for Jarry, allows one to perceive, that is, to be modified by the surroundings by virtue of one's perception of it. Living also means being perceived, in other words, to modify the surroundings. He proves his point by stating categorically, "Because and thus everyone knows that opposites are identical" (342, Jarry's emphasis). Perceiving and being perceived are equated.

The play of mirror-images is paramount here as it is in Caesar-Antichrist. When Being becomes Living, Being "syllogistically" becomes Non-Being since it ceases to be what it is. It follows that "To Live equals to cease to Exist" (342). This death or cessation of Being/Existing, devoid here of metaphysical anguish, will be made possible in two ways. First, by Being's own "sterility." Equated with Genius, Being, the explicitly superior modality—"Being is better than Living" (343)—is manifestly male, and is associated with ejaculation. Genius, or absolutely superior intellect, requires "ejaculation" to survive. Stimulated and swelled with blood, it spasmodically disseminates Thought which upon being acted out promptly ceases to Exist (as Thought). Likewise, the failure to ejaculate precipitates Being's death because of atrophy. Sterile or impotent Being gives rise to (inferior) Living. On the other hand, it is claimed that Being will also perish by explicitly homosexual debauchery as well as because of reading Literature. Being involves neither perceiving nor being perceived: it is spontaneously generated thought.

Action and Life, although inferior to Being and Thought, are, however, in Jarry's opinion, "more beautiful than Thought when consciously or not they have killed Thought. Thus, let us Live and by so doing we shall be Masters" (344). The act of murder thus defines the beautiful and is coextensive with mastery of life, thereby making possible the creation of one's own being. When Jarry writes that "every murder is beautiful" (344), he is taking as a model the murder committed in 1893 by Louis Lesteven, invoked to refute those who counsel living (342). What Jarry appreciated was Lesteven's theatrics, the artistic acting out of his sadistic crime and his subsequent prison suicide. Taking his life proved that his life (and death) were given shape and controlled by his own willpower.

There is some confusion regarding the role of writing in this philosophy of existence. At first we learn that by transforming his life into literature, a writer can save his Being from death in Time. Then, however, living one's life to the hilt is placed in opposition to writing. Jarry's turnabout stems perhaps from his personal surpassing of his theories by totally identifying his life with his art. This revolutionary phenomenon, a linchpin of modern art, was recognized immediately as an important break with the past by Jarry's successors. In *Anthologie de l'humour noir* the Surrealist André Breton wrote, "Literature from Jarry on, takes place on mined ground. [. . .] We say that beginning with

Jarry [. . .] the differentiation long held to be necessary between art and life finds itself contested, ending with the total
destruction of the principle."[10] One notable consequence is the
concern of modern literature (and film) to reveal the process of
artistic creation as its very substance. Henceforth fictional and
dramatic characters, whether based on real people, mythological
or historical figures, or pure imagination, would frequently be
creators themselves: Cocteau's Orpheus, Proust's Marcel, Gide's
Edouard.

Pataphysics cleared the impasse which put thought on the side
of being rather than living. Thought, thus postulated, finds its
materialization on the bookshelves Jarry mentions in his essay.
The books live on while the writers succumbed to the mortality
of Time and Discontinuity. What was needed, a system of *lived
thought* in which thought could be experienced rather than merely
conceived, made it necessary to invent Pataphysics, a science that
could be lived.

The themes and images of *To Be and To Live* form a fundamental
network that informs Jarry's various writings. A triad of leit-
motivs takes on multiple meanings throughout: purity (sterility
or abstinence); debauchery (even when heterosexual, the female
is a specularization of the male); death (envisioned as a prerequisite
for omnipotence). Jarry's sustained treatment of death associated
with rebirth and power correlates to Pataphysics's essential paradox of fruitful destruction. This is clearly stated at the outset
of *Ubu Enchained,* when an exasperated Ubu admonishes his critics, "We shall not have demolished everything if we do not
demolish the very ruins themselves! However, I see no other way
to do so than to counterbalance them with some beautiful, well-
aligned buildings" (427). The pataphysician knows that destruction and construction are inseparable.

Some Consequences

The theoretical apparatus of Pataphysics spawned many visionary inventions, and, in fact, conventions. It renovated existing notions and launched them into the future: incipient

discoveries from "black holes" to deconstruction. It even helped revamp calendric time.

All of Jarry's characters operate according to the pataphysical principle of the exception, rather than the rule. In *Faustroll*, Jarry places this principle under the aegis of an ancient theory of matter, "clinamen," which accounts for the creation of life by a fortuitous chance collision of atoms, deviating from the line of their vertical fall, at an undetermined place and moment. Today, the concept has resurfaced in the field of quantum mechanics as Werner Heisenberg's uncertainty principle. Heisenberg, a German physicist and philosopher, proposed his theory of uncertainty, or indeterminacy, in 1927. It called for the substitution of a probability for a fixed orbit of a particle because simultaneous measurement of the position and momentum of a particle disturbs the system, so that there is always an uncertainty in the result.[11] Jarry interpreted the ancient Epicurean atomic theory (named "clinamen" by Lucretius) to mean that given this original chance occurrence, anything—and especially, any deviation—was possible. Above all, he saw it as a guarantee of free will and of individual freedom in general.

"Clinamen" is an absolute absurdity: logically, geometrically, mechanically, and physically absurd. The theory fascinated Jarry for this and other reasons. It is absurd and far removed from practical experience—indeed it cannot be obtained through experiments—and yet, it joins the virtual to the actual by means of defining the infinitely small: there is a close relationship between atomism and infinitesimal calculus. Moreover, "clinamen" is the smallest condition conceivable for the formation of a vortex, or of turbulence, at random in space and time. It is the smallest operator for rotation in the ideal flow, in other words, the inception of a spiral, the symbol of Ubu, ultimate turbulence and perpetual motion in a world of inertia.

In "Clinamen," a chapter in *Faustroll* (Book VI, chap. xxxiv), Jarry calls the notion "the unforeseen beast." He uses it to concretize his most bizarre cosmogonic hallucinations. First, he postulates the end of human civilization as a *fait accompli*. Amid the subsequent desolation, there remains only the Palace of Machines, in which a Painting Machine operates by means of "a system of springs without mass." According to the laws of pure chance, this "beast . . . ejaculated on the walls of its universe" (714) delirious scenes of a new cosmos. Pataphysics, seen in this perspective, is thus the ultimate mask, and literary sorcery, created to annul annihilation itself and to inscribe a textual absolute.

The laws of the pataphysician's "supplementary universe" also anticipate the modern scientist's concept of "antimatter" which presumes that "for every particle of ordinary matter, there is an 'equal-but-opposite' particle," such as the antiproton or the positron.[12] Not only does every particle have its counterpart inside the atom, but it also corresponds to a symmetrical particle in an unexplored universe, recognized by scientists as this one's double. With the pataphysical dimension of "ethernity," Jarry intuited the phenomenon of the "black hole," a universe capable of passing right through the earth. A black hole is "an assemblage of matter that has shrunk—more properly, collapsed—to a state so extremely dense that it has become invisible." Inside the black hole time and space would be interchanged, time slowed and light bent by intense gravity. According to black hole enthusiasts, "That other universes may exist is certainly possible. Each universe would have its own dimensions, its own physical 'constants' and laws. These universes would have their home in a 'superspace' indefinite in space and time."[13]

In fact, with his "Commentary to Help in the Practical Construction of the Time-Machine," Jarry plans the construction of a "time machine" which would explore time by means of space-exploring-machines.[14] The "Commentary" ingeniously speculates on the hypotheses and brilliant experiments of H. G. Wells's *The Time Machine*. To begin with, Jarry states that the present is three dimensional (735). Time thus becomes a sequence of solids. The ideal exploration of this "space" would require that the machine isolate us from time, that is, that we "remain immobile in absolute Space, along the Flow of Time" (736). Seen from the machine, the past is beyond the future. It follows that if we could close ourselves instantly in the machine (thus isolated from time and immobilized), the voyage into the past would "consist of the perception of the reversibility of phenomena. One will see the apple jump back from the Earth to the tree, or the resuscitation of the dead, then the cannon ball reenters the cannon" (742). This description rivals that of the formation of a black hole: "The 'arrow of time' will change direction. From the viewpoint of an observer outside the universe (although denied the ability to make such an observation), our lives would seem to begin with the grave and end in the womb."[15] For the machine, two pasts coexist: the real one and that *"constructed by the Machine* when it returns to our Present, and which is nothing but the reversibility of the Future" (742). Similarly, "to those inside the collapsing universe [—the incipient black hole—] time's arrow would appear normal."[16] In order to regain the real past after its journey through the future, the machine must traverse a point suspended between the future and the past, symmetrical to the real present, "that one should rightly call the *imaginary Present"* (742). Jarry deduces that, from the machine, time appears to be "a closed curved surface" (742–43). One of the "strange effects of black holes . . . [is] the tight curvature of space."[17] Ultimately, for the pataphysician,

Time is the transformation of a succession into a reversal
    That is to say:
THE EVOLUTION OF A MEMORY. (743)

The conscious pataphysician constantly seeks to surpass the here and now. Pataphysics, according to Jarry's definition, is "the science of what is superadded to metaphysics, either in itself, or outside of itself, extending as far beyond the latter as the latter goes beyond physics" (*Faustroll*, 668). Jarry's desire to escape metaphysics returns today, newly masked under the philosophical thrust of deconstruction. Its chief spokesman, Jacques Derrida, "shows the poles in the binary oppositional couples of metaphysics to be differed-deferments of each other, the same though different. Each pole is as much the other as it is 'itself'; hence each returns eternally in its opposite, 'is' its opposite. Each pole exists only as an in-between, an 'entre-deux,' not as an autonomous unconditioned entity."[18] Deconstruction attacks the problematic of

opposition in an effort to suspend the metaphysical structure of
polarity. Derrida's philosophy "invites us to undo the need for
balanced equations, to see if each term in an opposition is not
after all an accomplice of the other."[19] He would like to free
Being from the "traditional and metaphysical domination by the
present or the now."[20] The effect of the concept of the "same-
though-different" in Derrida's thought, parallelling the pataphysician's notion of "equal-but-opposite," is that "all the conceptual oppositions of metaphysics, . . . (signifiers/signified;
sensible/intelligible; writing/speech; speech/language; diachrony/
synchrony; space/time; passivity/activity, etc.) become non-per-
tinent."[21] Unlike Jarry, however, Derrida finds that "metaphysics, defined as a system of opposites, can never be escaped, because
to attempt to step outside metaphysics is to place oneself in
opposition to metaphysics, that is, to repeat it."[22] Whereas deconstruction offered a relatively pessimistic stance in terms of
surpassing binary structure, it is of considerable interest that a
new phase in the deconstructive process (begun with "A Question
of Style," an early version of *Spurs, Nietzsche's Styles,* presented
at a Colloquium at Cerisy-la-Salle in July 1972) brings deconstruction and pataphysics closer together. This new phase is
"affirmative" (Derrida's terminology) in its strategy of internally
subverting metaphysics. No longer only a question of reversal of
the metaphysical hierarchy, but of neutralization accomplished
by means of the emergence of a new hierarchy, in which new
concepts are circulated, affirmative deconstruction disrupts with
a new mandate of primacy and priorities. Affirmative deconstruction does not resolve the dialectics of metaphysics, nor does it
stand in dialectical opposition to metaphysics: it escapes the
economy of truth and/as the phallus. Its relation is *supplementary.*
Pataphysics, more overtly optimistic from its inception, structures will or desire toward the "supplementary universe." By so
doing, Jarry does not negate the metaphysical dualities, does not
step outside metaphysics in the sense of facing it from an external
vantage point. Very much in the same spirit as deconstruction's
"relays," "intersticies," "creases," and the like, by which one
infiltrates and subverts metaphysical hierarchies, Pataphysics's

task is continually to *displace* metaphysics, through translation (another important deconstructive tactic) to the Imaginary, the same atemporal, aspatial point the Time Machine must traverse.

Time, Jarry's favorite marionette, underwent more concrete changes by the devising of an uncommon calendar:

the Pataphysical Perpetual Calendar begins on Jarry's birthdate, September 8, 1873—the Feast of the Nativity of Alfred Jarry. Thus begins the Pataphysical Era (E.P.). That day is the first day of the first month of the year, Absolu. Each of the thirteen months has twenty-eight days with the exception of the month of *Gidouille,* which has twenty-nine. (The other months are *Phalle, Clinamen, Haha, Sable, Merdre, Pédale, Palotin, Décervelage, As, Gueules,* and *Tatane.*) One feature of this calendar is that the thirteenth of every month is a Friday.[23]

The calendar was the creation of the College of Pataphysics, founded on 11 May 1948, in recognition of the fiftieth anniversary of the writing of *Faustroll.*[24] Its members are all conscious pataphysicians. They acknowledge various precursors, such as Rabelais (an obvious inspiration for *Faustroll*) and Rimbaud, and successors—called "patacessors"—such as Julien Torma and Raymond Roussel. The College is neither exclusively devoted to Jarry nor is it a solely French association. More has been published on Jarry and his works, however, than on any other author, and the College clearly believes that any pataphysical organization cannot ignore him. Two years after its formation, the College began publication of the *Cahiers du Collège de 'Pataphysique.*[25] To honor the fiftieth anniversary of Jarry's death, publication of the *Cahiers* terminated with number 28 in 1957. Subsequently, the College published the *Dossiers.* The publication periodically undergoes a name change, but almost every issue continues to include some material on Jarry.

One of the more noteworthy of the College's meetings was convened to fête the nineteenth centenary of the exaltation of Nero to the Roman Empire. In 1953, the College organized an Expojarrysition in Paris, at the Galerie Jean Loize, rue Bonaparte. The documents exhibited contributed to a resurgence of interest in Jarry's works and substantially expanded the availability of manuscripts and correspondence for research. The March-April 1981 *Europe* is a special issue on Alfred Jarry. The healthy state of Jarry studies, to a great degree made possible by the ongoing efforts of the College, occasioned a ten-day colloquium devoted to Alfred Jarry and all aspects of his work, at Cerisy-la-Salle, under the auspices of the Centre Culturel International de Cerisy-la-Salle (27 August–6 September 1981).

Chapter Three
Long Live the King: Ubu

Intertextuality

The "Ubu phenomenon" offers a particularly apt example of intertextuality in Jarry's works. A comprehensive interpretation of the character depends upon an understanding of Ubu, not only as the gross and lunatic panjandrum of the Ubu plays, but also as a cauldron of complex aesthetic and philosophical passions. Ubu appears in seven important and diverse texts, indicating the consequence of Ubu in Jarry's literary universe.[1] "L'art et la science" [Art and Science], published in 1893, constitutes Ubu's official début. Unpublished versions of *Ubu roi* [King Ubu] and *Ubu cocu* [Ubu Cuckolded] existed, of course, with different titles, ever since the physics class of Monsieur Hébert inspired certain schoolboys to invent Ubu's ancestors.

Between the ages of twelve and fifteen (1885–88), Jarry composed several plays and poems, collectively titled (between 1897 and 1898, by the adult Jarry) *Ontogénie* [Ontogenesis]. Themes and images anticipate the Ubu texts. In *Les Antliaclastes* and *Bidasse et Compagnie,* for example, the scatological theme is paramount. The nascent character type, monolithic and overbearing, dominates. The adolescent Jarry already favored symbolic objects and machines—especially the sewage pump. His fondness for puns, neologisms, anagrammatic names, and use of archaic vocabulary was developing. All of these early works exhibit the style of the "potache," the impertinent and keen-witted schoolboy, clearly marking them as predecessors to the Ubu saga.

Throughout, the ostensible social, political, or familial frameworks of the Ubu plays serve as pretexts for an enactment of pure instinct, embodied by Ubu. Ubu surpasses his manifest repre-

43

sentation of an evil dictator or embezzler. He symbolizes absolute freedom from society's regulations. Like a child, Ubu can be engagingly repulsive. Amoral, he refuses bourgeois materialism but participates simultaneously in the sacralization of matter: both fecal and cerebral. He recognizes no law but his own bestial desires. The liquidation of socio-political structures clears the way for Ubu's libidinal preoccupations. Whether king, cuckold, or slave, Ubu's essential character remains unaltered, and his main concern is the satisfaction of his physical needs. To accomplish this he "expeditiously annihilates not only the existing order, but all possible order."[2] He represents, in a hyperbolic fashion, the grotesque of the real world and the hilarious but vitriolic revolt against it which paradoxically establishes the reign of the grotesque Ubu. Jarry describes the outlandish mongrel in "The Paralipomena of Ubu": "If he resembles an animal he has especially a porcine face, a nose like the upper jaw of the crocodile, and the total effect of his cardboard carapace makes him the brother of the most aesthetically horrible sea-beast, the horseshoe crab" (467).

Ubu personifies Jarry's favorite intellectual device: paradox. The creature is essentially double, the unstable juncture of the human and the inhuman. He upsets and disgusts his spectators who nevertheless find themselves rooting for this anti-hero. Speaking of Ubu's unique role in literary history, Micheline Tison-Braun writes,

His activity has no affective motive. It is beyond pleasure or pain, as it is beyond good and evil. It thus escapes the human. Ubu is an essentially modern robot. It is with this vision of the inhumanity in man and of the absurdity of society that the great century of humanitarianism closed, a century that had conceived, at the outcome of evolution, the saint, the genius, the hero, the superman.[3]

Appropriately, Ubu stows his Conscience in a suitcase.

The *"gidouille"*

Ubu's physical shape itself offers a key to his significance. A close relative of the sphere, he incarnates the synthesis and wholeness fundamental to pataphysics. Circles and spheres serve often, in Jarry's oeuvre, as metaphors for the self shielded in its pure, primeval essence from exterior vicissitudes. Ubu's sharply pointed head, however, in the shape of a cone, adds another dimension to his body. Sharpness, in Ubu's case, corresponds to the function of sadistic penetration.[4] Accordingly, *gidouille* combines frequently, in the Ubu texts, with *corne* ("horn"): "Cornegidouille!" is one of Ubu's pet expletives and is the first word he pronounces in "Puppet Show," *Caesar-Antichrist,* "The Paralipomena of Ubu," *Ubu Cuckolded,* and *Ubu Enchained.* It joins two basic aspects of Ubu: penetration and devouring in order to protect the self in the face of external reality. He penetrates others in order to extract the coveted substance and then consumes it inside his potbelly. His bizarre physical shape—combining horn and belly—mimicked by his speech, has further ramifications which are consonant with Ubu's identification with the hermaphroditic *bâton-à-physique.* He is androgynous, combining both male and female in a timeless union.

Seemingly drastic changes in Ubu's state, such as the shift from king, in *King Ubu,* to prisoner, in *Ubu Enchained,* are superficial. Where, after all, is free lodging and nourishment for Ubu's enormous *gidouille* to be found? In prison. Ubu, individualist par excellence, concludes, "I am beginning to establish undeniably that My Gidouille is larger than the entire earth. . . . It is it I shall serve henceforth" (461). In *Ubu Cuckolded or the Archeopteryx* the setting is the interior of the Gidouille, which has effectively become a universe. Any further expansion of its limits could have mortal repercussions: "We are digesting at this moment, and the slightest dilatation of our *gidouille* would cause us to perish instantaneously" (501).

While speaking of his spherical form Ubu adds, "Man, dazzled, genuflects before our Beauty, an unconscious reflection of our Sage's soul. And all must, respectfully, burn incense at our knees" (188). This self-attribution of perfection and divinity derives— like the symbolism of the sphere—from the insignia covering the *gidouille:* the spiral, symbol of dynamism and infinity. By arrogating divinity to himself, Ubu implies his self-creation. The

theme of self-creation, omnipresent in Jarry's works, and symbolized here by bold graphic means, corresponds to Jarry's cult
of subjectivity. His highly personal, elliptical, obscure writing
as well as his rejection of "reality" in favor of role-playing is but
the consequence of this central motif. In the sense that Père Ubu
represents the archetype of creation ex nihilo, he merits his name
of "Father."

Jarry's agile wielding of paradox allows the *gidouille* to simultaneously symbolize divinity and monstrosity. While indubitably
comical (and childish sounding) the *gidouille* also, and very concretely, puts on stage "that great metaphysical fear which is the
root of all theater."[5] On a more literal plane, this giant gut
symbolizes the processes of assimilation and rejection, construction and destruction, upon which all life depends. Indeed, according to traditional symbols, the *gidouille*'s spiral schematically
depicts the evolution of the universe. The Egyptian hieroglyph
of the spiral signifies "cosmic forms in motion, or the relationship
between unity and multiplicity. . . . The spiral is essentially
macrocosmic."[6] Egyptian iconography also considers the spiral
as an "attribute of power." "Spiral movements . . . may be
regarded as figures intended to induce a state of ecstasy and to
enable man to escape from the material world and to enter the
beyond, through the 'hole' symbolized by the mystic centre."[7]
Spirals and circles symbolize the realization of the Self, the con-
solidation of the inner being. Like the *bâton-à-physique*—with
which Ubu is equated in *Caesar-Antichrist*—a concise and powerful image, the *gidouille* is a masterly expression of the pataphysical realm.

"merdre"

The linguistic world of Ubu could be said to "disarticulate"
language. Ambiguity, puns, neologisms, clichés, and words used
for their morphophonetic rather than semantic content characterize that world. Ubu's instinctual, anarchic nature is translated
by an aggressive discourse that constitutes a revolt against traditional usages of language. On phonetic, lexical, and syntactic
levels, deviations from the norm abound. Words, for Jarry, func-

tion as "crossroads" (172) and as "polyhedra": the speech on the living *polyèdres* cultivated and studied by Achras in *Ubu Cuckolded* serves as a commentary on the operation of signs in this specific literary universe. The many-sided solids not only give birth to infinite offspring but are capable of revolting against Achras who must use physical force to keep them well behaved (495–96).

A lexical triad—*merdre, phynance,* and *physique*—underpins the Ubu plays. *"Merdre,"* the first word uttered in *King Ubu* (and the cause of scandal at its premiere), is a defiant child-like projectile hurled at the disdained order of the adult world.[8] Ubu deifies excrement, singing hymns to his *merdre*-pump. The addition of the "r" resulted in the creation of a talisman, a magical word that opens into a legendary universe. It is the word shouted by Ubu to signal his political coup. Written in capital letters, it symbolizes Ubu's egocentric and vulgar nature. A simple word suddenly became charged with mythic significance: *merdre* is not merely a play on words. As the most privileged entry in Ubu's lexicon, *merdre* is happily applied to people and objects in his universe, which really only exists in relation to Ubu himself: he addresses his officer as *"garçon de ma merdre"* and his wife as *"Madame de ma merdre."* Enamored of his *pompe à merdre* in *Ubu Cuckolded,* he informs his world with overflowing, obscene matter.

The erasure of "the word" from *Ubu Enchained* counterbalances its thunderous presence in King Ubu, extending the pataphysical principle of the equality of opposites to the construction of entire texts. By pointing out its absence in the opening dialogue—just as *"Merdre"* opened *King Ubu*—and not simply omitting all mention of it, Jarry signaled the word's continued importance.[9] Ubu enchained is the indissoluble double of Ubu enthroned. *Merdre,* initially a symbol of destruction, acquires a philosophical and conceptual value. Jarry, like the alchemists he admired, transmuted matter, making even of feces an extraordinary symbol of the union of opposites. A consideration of the term *merdre* exclusively in the domain of *King Ubu,* however, fails to reveal its full connotation.

By changing the spelling of *finance* to *phynance* the word's field of connotation is expanded in a similar fashion. It is a matter of

record that *phynance,* as well as *gidouille* and *merdre,* was part of
the original lycée creations revolving around Monsieur Hébert.
The fact that Jarry did not invent the terms does not alter the
ingenious *use* to which he put them. He attributed to them a
symbolic and philosophical significance they did not possess before he adopted them. Speaking of Jarry's interest in *merdre,*
Hunter Kevil maintains that "If we think of Symbolism as the
pursuit of the Ideal, [. . .] then shit, the obvious symbol of the
material world in which we are obliged to exist, is the Symbolist
substance par excellence."[10] In folklore, alchemy, and Freudian
psychology, a virtually worthless substance is often associated
with what is most highly valued.

The graphemic deformation allows the word *phynance* to signify,
first, odious exterior "reality" (represented in part in *King Ubu*
by the Financiers); second, the liberation from that world made
possible by Ubu (who forces the Financiers down the trapdoor
and proclaims himself Master of Finances); and third, *phynance*
refers to the substance Ubu abusively extracts from his subjects.
It becomes his essential nourishment. Whence the equivalence
of *phynance* to *merdre* and to *cervelle:* Ubu collects *phynance,* pumps
merdre, and gayly disembrains his subjects in a structurally identical manner. In fact, in *Ubu Cuckolded* the rallying cry of King
Ubu *("Merdre!")* is replaced by *"A la machine!"* referring to the
disembraining machine.

Physique, too, synthesizes the forces of Ubu's mythical existence. On the one hand, the word recalls the physics class that
engendered Ubu. Much of Ubu's discourse parodies Professor
Hébert's pedantic diction. On the other hand, the requirements
of Ubu's corpulent physique provide his sole motivation and
determine his movements with the décor. Ubu's language mirrors
his imposing shape and leaves room for no idiom but his own.
Even his crafty wife incorporates Ubu's vocabulary into her own,
speaking of "cauliflower *à la merdre."* And when Ubu moves into
Achras's house he also dispossesses Achras of his language. To
Achras's indignant complaint, "It is a manifest imposture," Ubu
exultantly responds, "A magnificent posture!" (497). Ubu's ultimate extraction and assimilation/deformation, that of another's

(all others) language, dehumanizes and virtually annihilates any opponents. Achras silently exits: language is power. All three, *merdre-phynance-physique*, combine with words connoting Ubu's sadistic nature. His sticks, hooks, pistols, scissors, and horns *à merdre* as well as *à phynance* and *à physique* serve as instruments of torture to extract payment and thus to procure him gastric satisfaction. Ubu himself indicates his military arsenal: "The Russians are not far away and we shall soon have to attack with our weapons, as much with *merdre* as with *phynances* and *physique*" (381).

Puppet Theater

Ubu was originally conceived as a puppet and was put on stage as such by Jarry and his comrades in 1888 in *Les Polonais* [The Poles]. Much later, in 1901, Jarry created *Ubu sur la Butte* [Ubu on the Montmartre Hill], which opened at the Quatre Z'arts theater in Montmartre, played by marionettes of the Gueules de Bois troupe. The play follows the scenic thread of *Ubu roi*—coup d'état, tyrannical reign, forced exile—with further schematization and simplification.

Jarry envisioned the *mise en scène* of the complexities of the Ubu character in terms of simplified décor and acting deriving from the theater of the marionette. In the case of *King Ubu*, it is partially from this interpenetration of the human (actor) with the inanimate (puppet)—to the detriment of the former—that the existential horror of the play results. Jarry's play is at the antipodes of the transcendent psychological and aesthetic laws of puppet theater, with which he was familiar.[11]

Ubu, giant and anchylosed marionette, is nevertheless made of flesh and bone. A human being gives him blood and breath. The confrontation of the two orders was judged intolerable by the original public. [. . .] Man made himself an object and a monster to mock his fellowman.[12]

From the marionette Jarry borrowed condensed action and the stylized character. The performance is timeless and symbolic; the aesthetic goal was approached by using masks. Jarry specified that "the actor will have to substitute for his head, by means of a mask enclosing it, the effigy of the CHARACTER." Thus,

the eternal nature of the character is included in the mask. [. . .] All those who have known enough to see a Puppet Show were able to verify them [the principal expressions of a mask]. As they are simple expressions, they are universal. ("De l'inutilité du théâtre au théâtre," 407–8)

Ubu's enormous *gidouille* and his pointed, one-eared, three-toothed head (with two horizontal slits for eyes) were barely supported by his tiny legs: whence his stiff tottering gait, similar to that of a monstrous puppet. Following Jarry's directions, Ubu's gestures were all acted like a marionette. But whereas the actual marionette theater miniaturizes characters—even monsters— *King Ubu* transgresses this law by enlarging them in order to "vampirize" the consciousness of the spectator. The action, in the illustrative *King Ubu,* proceeds directly from Ubu's conspiracy to murder of the legitimate king, to battle, to Ubu's flight toward France. In the manner of the puppet theater, Ubu orders enemies down the trapdoor and throws the toilet brush onto the dinner table. In imitation of the action and language characteristic of the theater of marionettes, in his travels Ubu repeatedly locks up his Conscience in a valise and words are often taken at face value. Tonality veers from the slapstick to the macabre to the tragic. Changes in symbolic psychological states (such as terror or disgust) rather than psychological verisimilitude correspond to the tension among tones.

To a large degree, Jarry's interest in marionettes derives from a desire to be rid of theatrical conventions, and above all the actor whom Jarry considered to always betray the poet. "Only marionettes, of which one is master, sovereign, and Creator, [. . .] translate our thoughts passively and in a rudimentary way" (422–23). He preferred a symbolic rapport with the "real" world and rejected a naturalist copying of it.

The décor as well as the acting of King Ubu conforms to the goals of condensation, simplification, and stylization: to that end, against an unchanging background a well-dressed character would enter, as in the puppet theater, in order to hang up a placard indicating the scene's location. (Notice that I am certain of the "suggestive" superiority of the written placard over the décor . . .). Suppression of crowds. [. . .] Adoption of an "accent," or better, a special "voice" for the main character. Costumes with as little local color or chronology as possible (which better renders the idea of something eternal). (1043)

Ubu, of course, never changes his costume. He indicates superficial changes in his condition by means of an accumulation of heteroclite props: stick, stakes, broom, crown, handcuffs, ball and chains, valise, umbrella, and so forth. The tangible leads directly to "irreality." The acting must therefore be simple, synthetic, and evocative; the décor symbolic, dynamic, and synchronic, the material extension of the psyche. Finally, the mise en scène, borrowing from the puppet theater, but deformed to suit Jarry's personal obsessions, verges on the metaphysical. Like Ubu, oaf and vampire, it is a tragicomic model of alienation.

Humor

Jarry extended the comic into the domain where anxiety impinges upon amusement. "Laughter," he wrote in a 1902 theater review, "is born from the discovery of the contradictory." A few lines further on he exclaims, "and the admirable logic of the absurd!" While he delighted in comic absurdity, Jarry obviously took the question of humor quite seriously: he recognized the need to apply the "technical and philosophical processes" capable of eliciting laughter. [13]

He reports having attended during his *lycée* years Henri Bergson's lectures detailing a theory of laughter. Jarry's "scientific" methods put to use that theory. Bergson's statement that "the comic expresses above all a type of particular inadaptation of a person to society" must have appealed to the adolescent. [14] Like a sociologist, Jarry describes the world by means of an increasingly detailed account of a specialized phenomenon. It is his oblique point of view and his "straight" delivery that make his descriptions humorous. He never participates in the effects he produces. His description of railroad passengers, for example, rests on a comparison with the caveman's instinct to enclose himself in caves. The willingness to enclose oneself in a "rolling cage" thus becomes a vestige of the habits of prehistoric man. [15] In another instance, affixing a postage stamp to a letter is, for the innocent observer, based on a superstition that, in order to communicate with friends momentarily far away, all one must do is

> throw into *ad hoc* openings similar to sewer drains, the written expression of one's tenderness, after having encouraged, by means of a donation, the very distressing tobacco trade, and acquired in exchange some small images no doubt blessed, that one devoutly kisses on the back. [16]

To cite another example, in a deft logical switch, Jarry explains that a Negro who left a Parisian café without paying, running head first into the waiter's stomach as he fled, was in fact an African explorer tasting local products for scientific purposes, and was merely greeting the waiter in the fashion of his native land. He was thus no more a common crook than the French colonialists. [17] Other Bergsonian comic devices were effectively employed by Jarry: the mechanical body or man seen as a marionette, the transfiguration of a person into a thing, mental or corporeal inflexibility, and blindness to the disharmony between life as it is and as it ought to be.

With what might be termed "lucid blindness" Jarry denied the very contradictions of which he was acutely conscious and proclaimed a synthetic worldview in which all things are equal. It has been said that Jarry was

> the first to give humor its full contemporary expression. Even more than that of Edgar Poe, Jarry's humor is metaphysical and mathematical; even more directly, it depends on the play of opposites. [18]

This play of opposites, the inadaptation of the individual to society, and existential anxiety are all intimately related. As André Breton intuited, the theory of comedy which best elucidates Jarry's oeuvre is Freud's; the tradition to which his humor belongs is that of "black humor." [19] There is, as Philippe Soupault wrote, "a spirit of vengeance" in Jarry's comedy, comparable to Shakespeare's; "Falstaff seems like Ubu's older brother."[20] In Freudian terms, humor results when the pleasure principle takes revenge on the reality principle. It is clear, Breton wrote, that Ubu is

the magisterial incarnation of the nietzschean-freudian id that designates the ensemble of unknown, unconscious, repressed forces, of which the ego is but the permitted emanation, entirely subordinated to prudence.[21]

According to Freud, humor is therefore liberating. It is also "sublime" and "elevated": the ego is triumphantly invulnerable, refusing to suffer because of external reality; the ego denies that the traumatisms of the real world can affect it; in a stunning reversal, the ego demonstrates that such potentially painful instances can actually be converted into opportunities for pleasure.[22]

The "black humor" that Jarry unleashes with Ubu allows the dark, hidden, primitive forces of the id, outlawed by society, to be exteriorized. Ubu is man's psychic double, referred to by Jarry as "ignoble" (416). He accomplishes the "rebellion against authority, a liberation from its pressures," of which Freud spoke when elaborating a theory of the joke.[23] Jarry praised a description of Ubu as representing "eternal gluttony, the baseness of instinct erected as tyranny" (416). Black humor derives from the triumphant release of man's repressed double. It is for this reason that the belly-laughs Ubu elicits are tempered by an uneasy titter. Like the clown, Ubu embodies man's transcendent potential, his liberty, but also his alarming inhumanity.

Writing about the humor in *King Ubu,* Jarry stated firmly that his public was wrong if it expected a funny play. The grotesque masks worn by the actors were intended to set the tone. Before the actor who played Ubu on opening night was hired, the director (Lugné Poe) wanted to rehearse the role as a tragic one. When theater critics disdainfully wrote that there was not an amusing word in the whole performance, Jarry rebuked the audience for not at all comprehending that "Ubu was not supposed to say 'witty things' as certain *ubucules* claimed he should, but stupid ones, with all the authority of a cad" (416). Ubu's nature

was, Jarry reminded them, continually and clearly reiterated by
his wife's comments: "What a stupid man!"; "He is really
imbecilic."

Ubu is tragicomic. He represents man's freedom and the powers
of transcendance associated with the mask, but also man's inhumanity (his stupidity and lack of sensitivity) and the anxiety
of being haunted and dominated by his double. The laughter
Ubu elicits emerges from the gap between the self and its double.
He is an anti-hero, a pariah—chased from Poland and imprisoned
in France—existing on a borderline. It is this vertiginous borderline which is translated aesthetically by using clowning, slapstick, and exaggeration to present a dead-serious and painful
existence. There is doubt projected on the very identity of man.
Laughter (or violent denial in the forms of boos and whistles)
counteracts man's mute terror before his cloven identity. Ubu,
the anti-hero, enacts the anguish of man, deprived of reference
points in a world gone mad. The comic force of organized delirium
resides in the power of deformation and disproportion that lead
the conscious mind astray.

Tragicomedy is a brand of humor destined to register absurdity
and alienation. Intelligible communication may not be taken for
granted in an existence perceived as precarious and unstable. The
genre disconcerts in a more nefarious and nihilistic way than
either tragedy, which includes a measure of glory and exaltation,
or comedy, where things turn out all right. This modern hybrid
is the crossroads where horror, terror, corruption, and nonsense
meet the lark of a personal liberation from conventions. It is the
encounter of extremes: delirium and hyper-lucidity. Logic may
be overemphasized, or its forms used to arrive at absurd conclu-
sions. The "receiver"—reader or spectator—laughs (or hollers)
because there is no appropriate response to the rupture of a coherent cosmic order. Certainly, polite applause and casual exit
are impossible.

It should perhaps be added that Jarry's view of humor and his
comic technique provide a substructure for many of his works
other than the Ubu Cycle. The most pataphysical response to the

divine Doctor Faustroll's compendium of knowledge, to his ludicrous ratiocinations, and to his false sophistry, is the monkey's eternal reply: "Ha! ha!"

Nowhere ("Nulle Part")

Ubu, former King of Aragon, Count of Sandomir, and Captain of the Dragons, seizes the crown of Venceslas, Poland's legitimate King, and goes on a rampage. The "Poland" of *King Ubu* is not the real geographical Poland. In his speech at the play's premiere Jarry specified that the action "takes place in Poland, that is to say Nowhere," and in the printed program wrote, "the curtain unveils a décor whose goal is to represent Nowhere, with trees at the foot of beds, white snow in a decidedly blue sky." He chose Poland because the country is "legendary and dismembered enough to be this Nowhere" or at least a questionable locale. Moreover, "Nowhere is everywhere, and above all the country where one is." Jarry states that while it may be a useless gesture to force Ubu out of Poland, since after eviction and flight to "France," he becomes Finance Minister in Paris anyway, what is of consequence is that an intelligent public consented to be Poles for a few hours (403). By that he meant the audience was willing to "suspend" reality in favor of Poland, a new dimension.

He did not want the setting to refer to facts or action, but to remain in the realm of the imaginary. His audience, however, did not unanimously opt for suspending the rules of a "well-made" play. Some spectators categorically refused—noisily interrupting the play or storming out of the theater at *King Ubu*'s premiere—to loosen their grip on reality. Additionally, Jarry overestimated certain critics' willingness to accept the type of theater he launched. Unconcerned with copying reality, with verisimilitude or propriety, Jarry wanted theater to be "a dream unfurling like mauve streamers."[24] Theater should imitate the logic of dreams, and should therefore employ symbolism, condensation, disconnection of images, and displacement; it should have an elusive, ephemeral and haunting quality.

Ultimately, "Nowhere" or "everywhere" or "anywhere" is a state of mind which banishes logic and reason in favor of dreams,

memories, and hallucinations. This aesthetic position was clearly
an important one. Jarry reiterated it by naming a character Pyast
in the hallucinatory "Haschisch Rap Session" ("Les Propos des
Assassins") of *Days and Nights*.[25] Pyast, a name Jarry cited the
opening night of King Ubu, is the real name of the original
Polish royal family, while the Pyast of *Days and Nights* is a poet.
Thus, the setting of *King Ubu*, the writing of poetry, and controlled hallucinations are mutually valorized. This phenomenon
is consonant with the transformation of "Nowhere" in *King Ubu*
to the interior of the *gidouille*, Ubu's gigantic cosmic gut, in *Ubu
Cuckolded or the Archeopteryx*.

If the décor of *King Ubu* was a single surrealistic stage set—
including a backdrop depicting various climate zones, small el-
ephants grazing on palm trees, the indoors and the out of doors—
its purpose was to invite each spectator to concentrate on which-
ever portion he felt drawn to during a given moment of the play,
thereby remaining psychologically accurate for everyone. Such a
suggestive, abstract setting was organized according to the laws
of reason only to the extent that a character would hang up a
placard indicating the scene's location. Placing the play's action
"Nowhere" means neither that Jarry wished to eliminate décor
nor destroy dramaturgic conventions for the sake of nihilism. He
went beyond the purest dramaturgy he knew—puppetry—and
created a new system of expression. His program of deconstruction
is reiterated by Ubu's pronouncement which serves as epigraph
to *Ubu Enchained: "Cornegidouille!* We shall not have demolished
everything if we do not demolish the very ruins themselves!
However, I see no other way to do so than to counterbalance
them with some beautiful, well-aligned buildings." In Jarry's
iconoclastic system of which the Ubu plays are but one example,
destroying destruction, negating what is already negative, dis-
membering what is already absent, equals creation of the highest
order.

"Ignoble Double"

At the Théâtre de l'Oeuvre on that infamous evening of 10
December 1896, Jarry said, "You are free to see in Monsieur

Ubu all the multiple allusions you wish, or a simple puppet, the deformation by a schoolboy of one of his teachers who represented for him all that is grotesque in the world" (399). Jarry must have uttered these words tongue-in-cheek, for in the program he gets more to the point: "Monsieur Ubu is an ignoble being, which is why he resembles (by the lower parts) everyone."

In response to those who refused to see any resemblance to themselves in King Ubu, Jarry published a vehement defense of his dramaturgy in *La Revue blanche* on 1 January 1897. In "Questions Regarding Theater" he explains that he could have easily presented an Ubu pleasing to the Parisian audience but that by observing decorum he would be committing a more despicable act. He intended the stage to be "like that mirror in the stories of Mme Leprince de Beaumont [an eighteenth-century novelist] where the vicious man sees himself with bull's horns and a dragon's body, in accord with the exaggeration of his vices; and it is not surprising that the public was stupified at the sight of its ignoble double who had not yet been entirely presented to it" (416).

For the artist, literary (or other) creation permits the expression of painful emotions and offers the possibility of transforming them into sources of pleasure, but that pleasure may not always be transferred to the spectator. The case of *King Ubu* is one in which certain viewers saw their fantasms symbolically enacted by someone else but could not derive pleasure from the spectacle. The manner in which Jarry portrayed unleashed libidinal energy was for some intolerable and turmoil interrupted the play for a quarter of an hour. The lead actor honked a horn to punctuate the audience's outbursts. Shouts and whistles countered laughter and applause. The battle continued immediately in the press reviews. Did they protest too much? Jarry analyzed the crowd's excessive reaction to the image of Ubu as their double: the crowd "got angry because they understood too well, no matter what they say about it" (417).

They understood, but denied, that Ubu incarnated their unconscious drives and most aggressive desires. *King Ubu* presented a ritual of psychic unveiling, forcing the audience to confront the images and the discourse of their unconscious. "A work of art or literature," writes Yvon Belaval in a preface to *Psychanalyse et critique littéraire,* "necessarily employs a comprehensible language—and one analyzable by the critic—because complexes and symbols, no matter how individualized they be, are types of universals."[26] *King Ubu* was perceived as a travesty: of a well-made play, of decorum, of verisimilitude, of respect for the audience. The play was a "travesty" in the etymological sense of the term, "to disguise": *trans* = "across"; *vestire* = "to dress." Ubu is meant to impose himself immediately by his vestments and mask. Before he can vociferate the fateful *merdre,* he stands on stage as the investiture of the unconscious in all its phallic glory. This "phallic being" refuses to be effaced. Ubu hides only when in mortal danger, reappearing ready to defend his Realm. Jean Gillibert, in a psychoanalytical study of disguise, remarks that "the parade of vestment in ceremonies signifies the investiture of the role and at the same time phallic fulfillment (the restoration of what is not shown)."[27] Ubu thus makes visible— restores presence to—the invisible or absent. He is a type of hieroglyph of the discourse of the Other. As such, he is not only a symbolic phallic representation but, by virtue of his costume, calls into play anguished dreams of disinvestiture, of exhibitionism. Gillibert comments on the "very great risk of profanation, of precarity" associated with ceremonial garb.[28] Paradoxically, the `disguise makes the "interior" visible and the "exterior" transparent.

Jarry told his audience that the mask has two functions. First, it depersonalizes the human actor so that he captures the "soul of the oversized marionettes" of *King Ubu.* Second, the mask allows the actor to be "quite exactly the interior man" (400). The fact that the play was hastily produced meant Ubu could not wear his special mask. Jarry decided that he sport instead a steel gray suit and a bowler hat, adding or subtracting his crown, royal cape, and other accessories as the scenes dictated, but always having a cane in his pocket. Michel Arrivé suggests assimilating this cane or walking-stick to the *bâton-à-physique* of *Caesar-Antichrist,* and thus introducing its symbolism into this play (Notes,

1169). The "mirror" presented to the original spectators was thus all the more unacceptable because their expectations of the reflected image of themselves so drastically conflicted with the deceptively dressed image in the mirror. In another paradoxical tour de force Ubu's disguise was "normal" attire: the travesty of travesty. Thus, the audience—informed by Jarry of the mask and its intentions—could not help but know that the character was its double. Jarry uses this unforeseen ruse of normality-as-disguise again in *The Supermale* where Andre Marcueil's bestial double comes into play.

Jarry's choice of words (in "Questions Regarding Theater") to explain his dramaturgy is revealing. He compared his stage set to a creature with bull's horns and a dragon's body. The horns symbolize power and combine into one object the male (penetration) and female (receptacle, cornucopia) principles. The dragon too is a universal symbolic figure. It "stands for 'things animal' *par excellence*," and is particularly associated with dangerous and aggressive animals. A symbol of instincts, the dragon represents, in Jungian terms, "the mirror of the unconscious." In alchemy, dragons fighting "illustrated the state of *putrefactio* (separating out the Elements, or psychic disintegration)." Hermetic doctrine places bulls and dragons on the side of darkness (they are the foes of sun-heroes) while the dragon by itself signifies "blind impulse toward gratification."[29]

The opening-night audience rejected the image of the self concretized in an omnipotent "fantasmatic" character, the very incarnation of the unconscious. It attacked this demiurgic creature endowed with dual gender, symbolizing the anguished regression to a time when the Self was not yet clearly delimited with relation to the Other.

Chapter Four
Double or Nothing

Les Minutes de sable mémorial: Haldernablou

The *Minutes* consist of sixteen individual texts (of which some are
further subdivided), additional pieces considered (by Michel Arrivé, editor of the Pléiade edition of Jarry's works) "relating to"
the *Minutes,* and the "Acte prologal" of *Caesar-Antichrist,* originally conceived as a finale to the *Minutes* under the title of "Acte
unique." Prose, poetry, and drama combine when Jarry dispenses
with narrative plot in favor of a web of metaphors and symbolic
actions. Add to this his acutely emotional and erudite language
and the enormity of the task of deciphering the *Minutes* becomes
apparent. There are, nevertheless, many themes and leitmotifs
common to the superficially diverse and disordered whole. Some
of the most salient include pederasty, the extensive influence of
Lautréamont's *Chants de Maldoror,* a Bergsonian development of
time, self-creation, and the supreme power of literature. Obses-
sive images occur of black sand falling in an hourglass, falling
raindrops, the foot walking and other cadenced movement, owls
and other phallic objects, and the eye. An analysis of *Haldernablou,*
one of the sixteen texts, makes clear that these elements are
further unified and subsumed by the privileged notion of the
double.

The "double" is a source of torment and fascination. By constructing images and characters symbolic of doubling, Jarry extends the pataphysical play of opposites to yet another level. This
dynamic spatialization of psychic dissociation and the tantalizing
but painfully impossible reunification within the textual universe,
underlie the valid but more extrinsic—pederastic and sadistic—
readings. In other words, Jarry's homosexual experiences and

literary idols served as his inspiration; however, the totemic exteriorization of his inner alterity and the playing out of his intrapsychic conflicts provide the matrix. And like their creator who projects his doubles into his literature, his characters systematically project their textual doubles, with devastating consequences.

Literary images, according to Freud, are expressions of desire. The literary work is itself a metaphor, always leading back to an absence. Jacques Lacan, applying the lesson of linguistics to Freudian theory, teaches that each word, referring to yet other words, is addressed to someone—be he silent or absent—and participates in the dialogue of the unconscious. Lacan calls this gap or lack in one's discourse "the discourse of the Other." It is precisely this "absence," this game of presence and absence, that bestows meaning. In Jarry's works, the phantasms of unfulfilled desires (represented by the literary work itself and specifically by the Other's role) generate new phantasms. This process, which occurs within the textual universe, produces "the Other of the Other," or "secondary" doubles. Such a return to the "same but different," to one's Other self and to Other selves causes anguish.

The title *Haldernablou*[1] joins the names of its characters: the duke Haldern and his page Ablou. In this sado-masochistic drama, homosexual love structures the fundamental doubling of the self. As J.-H. Sainmont points out, *Haldernablou* is a "sumptuous description" of Jarry's pederastic adventure with Léon-Paul Fargue. But he also compares Ablou to Valens, Sengle's fraternal double in *Days and Nights,* calling Valens the "phantom who haunts the hero and lives in him as if he existed externally."[2] Thus the double is an objectification of oneself that subverts one's subjectivity. Ablou is Haldern's "other" self.

Assimilation of the double remains impossible. Haldern's expression of love for Ablou, whom he knows he can never really possess, therefore takes the form of cruelty, and ultimately homicide, in order to punish Ablou in advance for his inevitable deception. There exists a Lautréamontian jealousy of the calumnious twin brother. Antonin Artaud—who not surprisingly

named his theater the "Théâtre Alfred Jarry"—described the type
of cruelty exercised between the two characters:

From the point of view of the mind, cruelty signifies rigor, implacable
intention and decision, irreversible and absolute determination.
[. . .] Cruelty is above all lucid, a kind of rigid control and submission
to necessity. There is no cruelty without consciousness and without the
application of consciousness. It is consciousness that gives to the exercise
of every act of life its blood-red color, its cruel nuance, since it is
understood that life is always someone's death. [. . .] And the sky can
still fall on our heads.[3]

The image of the stars falling from the sky symbolizes, in
Jarry's writings, the death necessarily subsequent to homosexual
passion. The act of love, become the apocalyptic and sadistic act
par excellence, demonstrates the inviolable taboo associated with
a unification of the self with its double. "The two friends," Noël
Arnaud writes of Jarry and Fargue, "dreamed of the impossible
love, yearning feverishly for that primitive androgyny [. . .] that
'adelphism,' fusion of two beings in pure love."[4] But thanks to
his own carnal advances, Haldern has sullied Ablou whom he
disdainfully considers impure and thus destined to be destroyed.
Erotic phantasms and dreams of power, characteristic of adolescent reverie, help transform a disappointing reality.

That Haldern's room is implicitly compared to his skull suggests that the nocturnal and funereal escapade takes place in his
own imagination. Death, consequently, signifies death of the
external world: upon Haldern's shutting of his eyes, an eye of
the skull opens. (In his description of the décor of Haldern's
room, Jarry specified, "Left wall: on a white pall, in a niche, a
monumental sculpted skull" [222].) Since in Jarry's iconography
the nyctalopic eye symbolizes Being and human creativity, the
opening of the clairvoyant inner eye, followed by Haldern's decision to kill the "beast with whom [he] has fornicated" (227)
indicates that the seminal penetration was, after all, an act of
inner creativity or self-insemination. To induce his meditation
on his "crime," Haldern commands: "Close the death of my
eyelids to the exterior world, so that I may reflect in the night

of the inside of my skull, a silence troubled only by the coughing pulse of the arteries of my spherical eyeballs." Following his order, the "Chorus passes as shadows in the obliquely pendular luminous projection of one of the skull's excoriated eyes that opens" (225). Upon "awakening" from his meditation, his gaze meets the skull's one-eyed gaze, likened to that of the Cyclops (227), whose eye evokes the idea of destruction.

Writing on *Les Chants de Maldoror,* Maurice Blanchot determined two principal propensities that evidently impressed Jarry who, at the time of composing *Haldernablou,* was reading the *Chants* with Fargue.

an extreme aggressive furor and an extreme somnolent passivity; contrary movements, but which do not really oppose one another. If furor implies desire to flight and the will to free oneself, this desire is "furious," i.e. it is not only a struggle against this evil or that "madness," but also evil and madness become means, passion of a struggle. And in the same way, passivity and somnolence do not represent a pure and simple abandonment to hypnotic forces; they are more a silent manner of fighting, a patient ruse, an ultimate possibility of revolt and of clairvoyance.

In the case of Lautréamont's work, it was also similarly "in the bosom of sleep that the metamorphosis was accomplished."[5]

In order to attain the proper state of meditation, that is, absolute subjectivity, Haldern enlists the help of his pederastically holy bestiary: bat, nightjar, toad, owl, trapdoor spider. In sleep, or absolute interiority, homosexuality and murder are equated, both related to a frenzy of intense emotion. In a Lautréamontian manner, Jarry equates immobility with motion and power. This paradox is sustained in the *Supermale,* where a locomotive and a cycle appear motionless since they advance at the same speed. Similarly, in *Absolute Love* the wings of Love are compared to the vitreous wings of moths moving so rapidly that they give the impression of fog. Haldern's passage into deep speechless meditation corresponds to the attribution of phosphorescent wings to the skull. The same tension characterizes the "frenzy" [which] is also sleep, this paroxysm [which] is immobility" of Maldoror's world.[6]

Like the opposition of the sleep and action of the lovers—noble and servant—and the sexual inversion which adumbrates the entire *Minutes*, the formal aspects of *Haldernablou* recast the theme of the double. A Prologue and an Epilogue frame two acts. The first act ends with the parting of Haldern and Ablou after their premonitory kiss. The second act denounces the "horror of the coupling of the double beast" (of which Jarry spoke in his 27 May 1894 letter to Vallette), although the actual copulation occurs off-stage. Jarry explained to Vallette that he selected the unconventional dual-name title in order to signify that horrifying union in one word. Jarry's reference to *"la bête double accouplée"* rather than to two animals coupling reinforces the notion of a single split being engaged in an act of self-love.

The Epilogue complements the Prologue. They are both situated in the funereal and sexually charged "triangular forest." The Prologue anticipates dawn while the Epilogue ushers the return of night. The voice of the Chorus wanes in the Prologue but reaches a shrill crescendo in the Epilogue. The voice of the Prologue's invisible Chorus is that of the settings and is highly symbolic of sexuality and death. The refrain, repeated in the Epilogue, continues the symmetry of the drama's alternations and equivalences: sex and death, day and night, love and hatred, lovemaking and murder. *Haldernablou* thus begins and ends with abstract, synthetic, and essentially fluid images; these permit the metamorphoses and the flow of time—symbolized by the falling sand of the hourglass—necessary for the exploration of man's inner potential. Indeed, Haldern imagines his ideal double, one who would not interfere with his all-important, completely self-oriented mental pursuits: "I would like . . . someone who is neither man nor woman nor entirely a monster, a devoted slave, and who could speak without breaking the harmony of my sublime thoughts; for whom a kiss were demonic debauchery" (216).

Days and Nights, Novel of a Deserter

Sengle, having been drafted, loses himself in reveries of Valens, his double, to avoid the misery of life in uniform. Sengle's homoerotic, narcissistic love for his fraternal double allows him to contemplate his own image projected outside of himself: Valens is Sengle himself at a younger age, imagined by Sengle as his younger brother. Their specularity, however, is not that of the cold and immediate reflection of a mirror. It is mediated by a curvaceous and fluid space that has replaced time. By abandoning the ordinary constraints of space and time, Sengle restructures his experience and thus, in a sense, creates it and controls it. Through such timeless, absolute self-consciousness, Jarry suggests, man creates his own perfection.

Images of fluidity therefore characterize the emergence and the presence of the double. In Sengle's case the medium is hashish and the effects are hallucinatory: "The land of hashish is in the room now, *brought back* by the lunar train. The air is pure glycerine, and similar to the way continents are encircled on geographical maps, Sengle and the three all have fluid halos twelve centimeters thick around their bodies" (824). The drugged state, explicitly a superior one, is not surprisingly Sengle's normal condition. Jarry equates Sengle's hallucinations with lucidity: the recruit thus takes notes during the séance (824).

In "The Cyanic Dream," the novel's third of five books, Sengle stands opposite the common man with day-vision who sees only the known. The book's first chapter alludes to *Confessions of an Opium Eater* by Thomas de Quincy,[7] as does the chapter "Consul Romanus" of Book II, "Book of My Brother." In the opiate dream of Quincy, the enunciation "Consul Romanus" caused the sudden appearance of the tunic-clad Consul in the midst of an English celebration one thousand years after the Roman Empire's zenith. Sengle compares Valens to the Consul. The ability to live simultaneously two moments separated in time clearly intrigues Sengle: to do so is to "authentically experience a moment of eternity, of all eternity, since it has no individual moments" (768).

Hoping to be discharged from the army, Sengle manages to take a strong dose of caffeine and be admitted to the military hospital, where he hallucinates that he ate silver nitrate crystals: "The cyanic blue radiated from his stomach to his skin like a black sun toward the circumference of the sky; his cold feet and hands harbored the heraldic azur . . . " (786). The hospital, naturally, became a favorite hideaway. In an untitled text related to the novel, Jarry explains, "I am in the hospital, therefore a poet" (839). In Sengle's opinion, the hospital is the army's gayest building: no uniforms and freely dispensed drugs. It is appropriate, then, that the hashish séance ("Les Propos des Assassins," Book V, chap. 4) takes place in the office of Nosocome, the hospital resident who befriends Sengle. The hallucinations and the irrational dialogue of the participants create an eternal present—"we shall never go beyond today" (822)—in which two distinct, even contradictory experiences may occur at the same time: one can be in the shade and the light or in fire and water. Time and space undergo a "cinematographic accommodation" (823) to their surroundings.

Although there is no specific reference to Valens in the "Propos," the concept of the double is manifest in several ways. First, the German philosopher Herreb (whose name resembles a German transposition of "Monsieur Eb," Ubu's predecessor), one of the "Assassins"—"assassin" and "hashish" derive from the same Arabic word—becomes "the man of the woods" under the effects of the drug, and proceeds to cut the others lengthwise in two (a motif repeated in *Caesar-Antichrist* [291] and in *Ubu Enchained* [457]). Second, by naming another participant Pyast— the real name of the Polish royal family—Jarry meant to situate the dialogue outside of measurable time and space and inside the Ubuesque world of Poland, in other words Nowhere (*"Nulle Part"*). Third, the imagery of the "Propos" is replete with Jarry's symbols of homosexuality, many of which were also incorporated into *Haldernablou*. The foot has indirect sexual significance since it is associated with walking, Jarry's metaphor for pederasty, and one used several times in the "Propos." He compares the agitated

"Assassins" to Wandering Jews, condemned to walk without rest until Judgment Day.

The dense meshwork of such imagery in the "Propos" intertwines many of Jarry's preferred symbols. Sengle, when approached by Herreb brandishing a wooden beam, reacts by raising his arms to eye level and projecting his spread fingers toward his adversary's eyes. The effect is immediate: Herreb's outcry of being penetrated by green nails combines two images associated with creative phallic sexuality. The chameleon (a literary symbol representing Léon-Paul Fargue in *Haldernablou*) and especially its eyes are characterized as green. Throughout Jarry's oeuvre green and greenish tints symbolize sex, death, and creation: "And the caresses of his hands on my white satiny skin permitted the green serpents of the spasms to convulse" (233). Nails, too, symbolize death: those who undergo homosexual death have their eyes nailed shut. Herreb notably ends up with a nail in his foot; a walking nail had been equated to a corn that could be cured by a horizontal bar, reminiscent of the *bâton-à-physique* (824). Indeed, it is the *bâton* or walking-stick that, like a magic wand, renders Herreb "man of the woods" (825). The "cure" made possible by the potent object, it would seem, is the autotransformation into one's double. The fact that the double is depicted here as "the man of the woods" reconfirms the notion suggested, for example, by instinctual Ubu or the Indian (in *The Supermale*) that this process corresponds to a regressive movement toward a more primitive stage of psychosexual development.

Another commanding image (further developed in *The Supermale*), the locomotive, epitomizes Jarry's interest in mechanization. Such reduction of intense emotions to pure physical force accounts for his portrayal of women as dolls whose speech is merely "wails of the thorax" (*Haldernablou* 216), and his description of people as "mannequins" (*Haldernablou* 220). He develops this motif with Ubu's henchmen, the half-human Palotins, with the "inorganic siren" of the phonograph, and finally with the locomotive. In the "Propos," Nosocome simulates the rhythmic noise of a train by jumping in place. Sengle's imaginary train brings back the "land of hashish." Because of undischarged sexual

tension, machines—especially the phonograph and the train—
have the ability to hypnotize.[8] The metallic cruelty and inflexibility of the phallic, penetrating train, combined with its power
to entrance, establish its identity with the double. This is the
hostile component of narcissism projected upon the double; it
endows him with terrifying and anguishing aspects. Significantly,
after the conclusion of the séance, Sengle composes a letter to
Valens.

Ill-adapted to army routine, he is thus a "deserter" in more
than one sense of the term: his desertion is military, narcotic,
and psychological. While his regiment—with Sengle present—
practiced their maneuvers, "Sengle was completely asleep and
was walking in the meadow for himself alone" (765). Jarry's
disdain for the military (which he felt demanded blind obedience
and constant submission, and worst of all, suppressed intelligence
in favor of brute force [763]) was based on firsthand experience.[9]
In spite of and because of the intolerable monotony and confor-
mity of army life, the "hypersensitive" Sengle felt obliged to
follow the "noble instinct . . . the instinct to keep one's self
intact and to maintain one's individuality impenetrable to exterior
forces" (763). Sengle escaped the "brutalizing degradation" of
the military by means of his dreams. After learning the date of
his conscription—"Sengle, free, is condemned to death, and he
knows the date" (749)—Sengle dreams of a walk he took with
Valens during which he felt as if he had smoked hashish:

His body walked beneath the trees, material and well articulated; and
something unidentifiably fluid flew above, as if a cloud had been an
icy mirror, and it must have been the astral being; and something more
tenuous was shifting more toward the sky three hundred meters away,
perhaps the soul, and an imperceptible string linked the two kites.
   "My brother," he said to Valens, "do not touch me, because the
string will get caught in the trees [. . .] and it seems to me that if
that happened, I would die."
   And he had read, in a Chinese book, an ethnology of a people foreign
to China, whose heads could fly up to the trees to seize their prey,
connected by the unwinding of a red ball of string, and then return
to fit into their bloody collars. But should a certain wind blow, the
cord would break and the head would fly back overseas. (749–50)

This vision of his astral self attached tenuously to his terrestrial self and the image of his head detached from his body, both under the aegis of a stroll in the woods with Valens, translates an obsession with the double. The comparison of the experience to a drugged state marks it as exceptional. The "astral body" holds a special fascination for Jarry, who adopted the tripartite theory of man expounded by occultists. [10] The fact that it fluidly and freely traverses space glorifies the spatial at the expense of the temporal: past and future need no longer be distinct. [11] Sengle's psychic dissociation becomes concrete in the image of his two bodies, his detached head, and his projection of Valens, his powerful, immortal double. The process of doubling in *Days and Nights* negates Sengle's weakness and spatializes an identity not subject to the flux of reality: Valens's name denotes "strength." Valens permits Sengle to escape the crushing reality of societal conventions, substituting a coherent and fulfilling existence in the place of psychosocial persecution. It is a question of transvaluation between Sengle and his double in a spatial modality.

Sengle's creation of Valens is concomitant with a subversion of time, specifically the opposition between day and night, whence the novel's title which combines the elements of time and desertion. The contrast between solar and lunar hours suffers a definitive destruction. Not only does day become night and night day, but the day and night of Sengle's imagination utterly confuse all standard notions of chronology. The novel opens with events that occur during the night: Sengle's efforts to achieve absolute fatigue through heterosexual sex in order to fail his army physical; the chapter's title is, however, "First Day." The second chapter's title, "First Night," is equally perplexing since Sengle's physical for the draft board must have taken place during the day. Thus, for Sengle, "normal" day and night are reversed. In addition, Sengle dreams during the day—to escape reality—and functions lucidly at night. His dreams become his only reality. The third chapter, "Other Day," plays with these new standards, creating the "day of Sengle's night," that is, the period when Sengle dreams lucidly, as he did during the soldiers' maneuvers.

"Dream" time neutralizes the distinction between day and night, past and future: Sengle

did not at all distinguish his thoughts from his acts nor his dream from his waking state; and perfecting the Leibnizian definition, that perception is true hallucination, he did not see why one could not say: hallucination is a false perception, or more exactly: feeble, or entirely better: *foreseen* (*remembered* sometimes, which is the same thing). And he especially thought that there are only hallucinations, or only perceptions, and that there are neither nights nor days (despite the title of this book, which is why it was chosen), and that life is continuous. . . . (794)

In exchange for his assurance of allayed anxiety and escape from the rigors of the uniform, Valens controls Sengle. One of the cardinal rules of the double requires that no physical contact taint his purity. The love Sengle denies women—associated with impure sexuality—is channeled into platonic friendship with Valens, the image of himself: "the word Adelphism would be more just and less medical than uranism, despite its exact sidereal etymology. Sengle, not sensual, was capable only of friendship" (769). Sengle prides himself on his absolute chastity. Evidently, his sexual exploits with women are incommensurable with homosexual activity. Probity in masculine relations defines his chastity.

Sengle suffers the consequences when he attempts to materialize his double and to become one with him. He "loses his head," so to speak, and the metaphor of the head/kite becomes all too real. Insanity is the penalty for trying to bring the pure, continuous world of the spirit into the discontinuous material world: Sengle could not become his double without first destroying him (763). Sengle's effort to capture Valens in a plaster head and to kiss the mouth-become-flesh leads only to a double fratricide (835). The plaster fell off the wall, hitting Sengle violently on the head and causing permanent damage: Sengle "groped in the dark night toward his missing Self" (835). "He destroyed Valens and Valens destroyed him. His dream is ruined forever. The sexuality that he rejected and that he did not know how to harness would henceforth render it impossible, no longer by dominating his senses, but the reverse, by the outrageousness of imagination."[12] Days and nights must also undergo further conflation. Sengle enters the "night of his night," that is when his dreams forfeit their lucidity.

The relationship of Sengle and Valens is parodied by an infratext, "Amber," a prose piece written by Officer Vensuet, where erotico-symbolic discourse caricatures the experience of doubling. In this case, the plight of two lesbian sisters adrift in a violent sea offers useful insights into Jarry's manipulation of the double. Separated by their father's trident, Phoebe (one of the sea-nymphs) is imprisoned on an island surrounded by glass walls, while Cymodocé (her sister) is thrown into the deep, suspended by her hair.

The story takes the form of a letter written by island-bound Phoebe to Cymodocé. She seals her letter in an amphora that a sea-eagle will carry off. The letter in the amphora, the lesbian sister on the walled island, and the amber formed deep within a whale's barrel-shaped body (comparable to Ubu's) respectively symbolize—and establish equivalence among—the written word, the double, and a mysterious, precious substance. All three (Word, Double, Jewel) eventually emerge from confinement. The double is also linked to the written word in the form of an inscription on the glass wall. The message addresses someone who "passionately kisses the Double through the glass," and for whom "the glass comes alive at one point and becomes a genital, and the being and the image make love through the wall . . ." (790–91).

Throughout the text tension exists between images of sexuality and of the desire for sublimation, that is the substitution of a nonsexual goal for a sexual one. This process of desexualization of libidinal energy is recognizable in the symbol of the soaring eagle. The bird's flight expresses the "dynamic desire of elevation and of sublimation." Winged flight is associated with air, "celestial substance par excellence," and symbolizes a "psychic aspiration toward purity."[13] The link between sublimation and writing is significant; an eagle carries off the inscribed story. The upward movement of the bird and the buoyancy of the amphora also characterize Phoebe (specifically in her desire to escape from the island and to reunite with her sister) and the jewel offered by the whale to the sea's surface.

Eventually, the floating body of Phoebe, recovered by her sister, is equated metaphorically to rare, buoyant ambergris issuing from intestinal secretions of sperm-whales (not unlike *merdre* from the *gidouille*). This is an appropriate symbol of the double emerging from the depths of a violated Self, and creating a sacred domain of irrational space, represented in the Lieutenant's "Prose" by ovoid shapes (turtle eggs, ship's hull, glass-walled island, vase, belly, amphora) associated with menacing—female—aquatic depths.

The thematics of the island, as illustrated in this tale of sapphic desire, is important because it underscores the homosexual structures of the narcissistic libido at work in the novel. For psychoanalyst Janine Chasseguet-Smirgel, "the island, surrounded on all sides, from which there is no evasion, represents the absolute anal mastery (utilized to defensive ends) that the subject excercises on the object tightly restrained in the ring of the anal sphincter."[14] In *Caesar-Antichrist* the anal sphincter appears explicitly in the form of the heraldic emblem Orle, a character who is clearly more important than his limited role in the play might suggest. "Orle" is the subtitle of the "Heraldic Act" in which Caesar-Antichrist cedes to the reign of Ubu, and the character plays the "closed ring of a vile sphincter" opposite Caesar-Antichrist-as-Phallus (287).

Between this act of *Caesar-Antichrist* and the following, subtitled "King Ubu," the stage directions indicate that "whales appear at the sea's surface." This imagery and symbolic movement prefigure (by two years) those of "Amber" in *Days and Nights*. In the latter it is no longer the whales themselves that surface but the jewel fabricated, according to the text, by their lovemaking. It is not surprising that Orle should be transmuted into the symbol of the island which functions as an unconscious image of the anal sphincter. In the case of the lesbian sisters, the island is the resting place of the dead Micromegas, referred to as "the giant man."[15] Phoebe loves the "dead giant of whom and on whom it is written in Ionian letters that it is astonishing to see that this large body stays stretched out in a small island" (790). Overlaid onto the story of the sisters, the coupling of the "giant dead man" and the "small island" (the large male buried and stiff in the restricted circle) adds a decidedly anal-sadistic and masculine homosexual aspect to the creation of the precious amber.

By means of a complex series of metaphors, the island is equated to the whale, metamorphosing into a vase when its crystal wall cracks and allows sea water to enter. The oval hole in the glass, at once sharp-toothed (a switch to oral sadism) and a "wound," is likened to the blow-hole of the whale. The jagged glass cuts Phoebe, covering her belly with blood to match that covering her fingernails: trying to escape and rejoin her sister, she desperately scratches at the "terrestrial silver mirror-backing of the window on the other side of the sea" (791).

It is clear the double is one's Other, one's image not reflected in a pool of water but on the *other side* of the water's surface. This implied configuration of (paradoxical) duality-in-unity explains the quadruple reference to the columns of Herakles: the island's itinerary leads it slowly toward these two pillars, the equivalent of those of the Latin Hercules, or the Jachin and Boaz columns of the Cabala. They constitute a "symbol deriving from the great myth of the Gemini."[16] This third sign of the Zodiac, the figure of all symbolic twins, has two manifestations. It is apprehended either as a fusion of opposites into "Oneness," depicted by the sphere (cf. Ubu); or as a split into conflictual or dissident opposites, represented by two-headed Janus or triform Hecate. "Amber" is clearly under the sign of the split twin. Hecate (also a symbol of evil femininity responsible for obsession and lunacy) appears in the story in the form of a priestess dancing around the island.[17]

The island's movement indicates the dynamic aspect of opposites rather than integration into a perfect being. The dual columns connected by a rainbow are another form of the inverted image of the double split by the water's surface. The rainbow possesses the strange power to change the sex of those who pass beneath it. In this particular form and function the columns and rainbow recall the image of the hourglass (fundamental in *Les Minutes de sable mémorial*), which is an avatar of the image inverted beneath the sea's surface. Because of dynamic polarity—inherent in the aspect of the Twin manifested in "Amber" (and in *Days and Nights* as a whole)—"the world of phenomena becomes a system of perpetual inversions, illustrated, for example, in the hour-glass which turns upon its own axis in order to maintain its inner movement: that of sand passing through the central aperture—the 'focal point' of its inversion. The Gemini, in essence a symbol of opposites is, in its dynamic aspect, then, a symbol of Inversion."[18] The center of the rainbow supported by the two columns is identical to the focal point of the hourglass. Here the "inversion" is explicitly sexual: specifically, in the terminology of psychopathology, "inversion" signifies homosexuality. Indeed, Cymodocé watches the island advance toward her, suspended by her greenish tresses from a point between the two columns of Herakles. Homosexuality operates on two levels in the text: first, the tale literally recounts the mutual love of two members of the same sex; second, this relationship refers to symbolic twinship or doubling of the self.

As long as he is permitted to exist independently, Valens functions as a friend and provides Sengle (whose name derives from "singulum: without having left me all alone" [747]) with an escape from solitude. By creating his powerful companion, Sengle negates the boredom and emptiness of daily life. In an effort to "preserve" his Self, he paradoxically expands himself, goes beyond himself, and engenders a tragicomic, hyperbolic world of "lucid delirium." Sengle, however, does not content himself with that world and pays the consequences. He loses his Self (the mouth of Valens's mask drinks his soul, in a manner similar to the exchange of being between the women in *Absolute Love*) and thereby his lucidity, a loss which for Jarry was analogous to death. Shattering the barrier separating the fragments of the self results only in permanent damage since love of the double expresses the impossible desire to unite one's fragmented self.

Ultimately, Jarry's philosophy presumes that the psyche can never exist as a coherent entity.

Countless primitive societies, folklore, and modern superstitions posit the soul as the equivalent of a second body or alter ego (or mirror-image). In *The Double, A Psychoanalytic Study*, Otto Rank describes the two main defenses against narcissism, or self-love, in the form of love of one's double, whatever its manifestations: on the one hand, "fear and revulsion before one's own image"; on the other hand (and the most common reaction) the loss of the shadow-image or mirror-image or soul.[19] Sengle has a fear of mirrors (753), and when he does look into his mirror, he rereads "the story of Sisyphus" (816). Discussing the essence of the tragic, André Green constructs two models of reversal or peripeteia. In the first, the "hero of the tragedy is fortunate, his desire seems to have a chance of being realized, he is on the side of the phallus, the possessor of power, of objects of *jouissance*." The reversal precipitates his fall. In the second model of the tragic, the hero begins "deprived of honors and pleasure, and is a pariah in the city; the development of the tragedy will see him overcoming many difficulties, appearing to prevail over the curse impending on him. Yet, like Sisyphus, his efforts will be in vain and he will rush headlong again down the slope to disaster."[20]

A descent into madness and suicide frequently combines with pursuit by the double who personifies narcissistic self-love, and specifically fixation in an early phase of ego development.[21] Connected with this are two factors clearly at work in Sengle's relationship to Valens, one of which is homosexuality. Rank writes that "the homosexual love object was originally chosen with a narcissistic attitude toward one's own image" and that "the double is often identified with the brother."[22] The other factor is the narcissistic wish to remain eternally young. Sengle's fear of aging, manifested in the novel by his creation of a brother who is forever young (Valens), expresses a "fear which is really a fear of death." The death of the double is thus, unconsciously, suicidal.[23] The butterfly which in psychoanalytic terms symbolizes rebirth, further illustrates the motif of the youthful double: Valens's soul is "a large brownish blue butterfly" (834).

After Sengle sees himself as Sisyphus, he closes the two panels of his mirror to cover his image in the third. The two outer panels are likened to wings and to hands: the connotation of this action becomes clear in *The Other Alceste* (see the next section of this chapter). Butterflies endure torturous treatment in other texts, for example, in *Absolute Love* where a sleeping Miriam is compared to a butterfly pinned down and labelled. On a semiotic level, the first syllable of *papillon* ("butterfly") repeats the word *pas* (the second component of a negation): "Je ne veux pas . . . pas . . . papillon!" (946). Thus, love of the double also implies pain and the negation of the self. As Rank aptly observes, the "fable of Narcissus combines the ruinous and the erotic."[24]

Sengle and Valens present a special case of doubling. Four of Jarry's five major doubles (Ubu, Faustroll, Emmanuel God, and Marcueil) are "powerful": they nullify a painful existence and incarnate a powerful Other. Ubu, for example, symbolizes instinctual drives while Faustroll represents the pataphysical quest for unlimited knowledge and Emmanuel God the desire for absolute love. Marcueil fulfills the wish for inexhaustible virility unlike Sengle who alone constitutes a weak double. Rather than offer the possibility of letting the Other speak freely, Sengle exaggerates the negative magnitude of repressive reality. Officer Vensuet's parody ("Amber") of Sengle's torment accomplishes within the novel the same exaggeration as the production of Sengle himself vis-à-vis ruinous, debilitating conventions (personified by the story-writing Lieutenant).

Vensuet writes poetry as well as prose. Sengle pronounces his superior's poem "officers' verse" just as he dismissed "Amber" with the disdainful "officers' prose" (758). Entitled "Pastorale," the poem has certain similarities to Jarry's *The Beloved Object, Pastoral in One Act,* and especially calls to mind the pathetic and ridiculous deformation by Monsieur Vieuxbois of his beloved's delightful song. Compare "Regardent vibrer l'air aux trilles du gazon" from "Pastorale" to "Perle son trille:/Comme il gazouille" (the Beloved Object's refrain) and "Perle son trouille/Comme il gazille!" (her suitor's deformation). Two lines from "Pastorale" also correspond to two poems in *The Revenge of Night:* "Rain of

War" and "X" (the number 10). "Le tonnerre tombant tintamarre ses tôles" ("Pastorale") alludes to "L'ours a tonné le gong tinta-marrant des fasques,/Et voici les démons dormant sous les ton-nerres" ("Rain of War"); the closing line of "Pastorale" duplicates the opening line of "X": "L'ivoire courbé pair au front bas des taureaux." These intertextual references suggest humiliation and fear and link them to the active, dangerous phallus. They also make clear the importance of an apparently insignificant portion of the novel.

Vensuet, subsequent to his poetry reading, tries to persuade Sengle of his own literary acumen. He professes admiration for Pierre Loti's *Le Livre de la pitié et de la mort*. In a chapter of *Faustroll* dedicated to Loti, Jarry demolishes—linguistically and ideologically—Loti's text. Sengle launches into a long description and defense of pantomime; Vensuet feigns comprehension. Sengle flees this mediocre mind, compared to "an old lady," who knows "art history and Latin quotations and vague ideas" (760). The vignette "Visiting the Old Lady" in *Love Goes Visiting,* makes clear that Sengle considered the Lieutenant vulgar and grotesque.

Both the poem and the prose piece function in the same way. They incorporate into the fabric of the novel a hyperbolic negative value system of weakness, psychic and physical pain, mediocrity, vulgarity, pretension, and so forth, manifested in the super-sym-bol of military authority so detested by Jarry. In stark opposi-tion—stylistic and semantic—stands "Hashish Rap Session," written in dialogue and highly theatrical. Jean Gillibert theorizes (citing Freud) that when one has suffered unbearably, one can no longer sublimate. The only way to hang on, the life-saver, is to "theatricalize" one's life. Another game must be substituted for the "game of the world": theatricality.[25] During the hashish séance, the voice of the Other speaks unfettered. This dramatic episode signals the passage from Sengle to Valens, whose name connotes power, strength, value, and courage. Valens, then, plays the same role—a double of power—for Sengle as Ubu, Faustroll, Emmanuel God, and Marcueil fufill for Jarry, and, in a general sense, the same role as the act of writing itself. Significantly, during the rap session, Sengle takes notes, that is, he is the scribe for the experience of provoked hallucination, of the theatricalized emergence of the Other.

L'autre Alceste [The Other Alceste]

With this "drama in five narratives" (first published in the *Revue Blanche,* 15 October 1896), Jarry rewrote Euripedes' play, changing the cast and substituting his own Alceste for the original. The "real" Alceste was the devoted wife of Admetes, King of Thessalia, an Argonaut and hunter of the wild boar Calydon. Admetes protected Apollo for nine years after the latter's expulsion from heaven by Jupiter for having killed the Cyclops. As repayment, Apollo arranged to have his host granted immortality on the condition that someone close to him be sacrificed in his stead. Alceste was chosen. Hercules, another house guest, managed to free her from Hell.

Jarry repopulated the myth with personalities from the Hebraic-Koranic tradition: King Salomon; Balkis, Queen of Saba; Doublemain, Death's monstrous ferryman; Salomon's son Roboam; and the Vizir Assaf, the King's minister. By telling the story of the *Other* Alceste, Jarry merged the Greek with the Semitic in order to abstract certain qualities of the principals. At issue are the necessity of Salomon's completing the construction of the Temple of Jerusalem, Balkis's subsequent self-sacrifice, and the insufficiency of the female as a substitute for the male. Although it is not mentioned in the drama, it would not have escaped Jarry's attention that King Salomon was also reputed to have murdered his brother. For *The Other Alceste,* like *Haldernablou* and *Days and Nights,* narrates the allegory of the double.

King Salomon is going to die but must remain alive one more year so that the demons working on the Temple will complete the task. His minister Assaf suggests that he replace his cedar cane with an indestructible golden staff so that, his soul departed, worms could not eat away his support and he could remain erect, thus duping the laborers. The prophet refuses to "prevent the worms from refuting an eternal lie" (909). Worms, a frequent image in Jarry's writings, traditionally symbolize homosexuality.

Assaf decides to trick Death by sending both a soul and an astral body that belong to someone else, namely Queen Balkis. The drama focuses on the journey of her astral body between the worlds of the living and the dead. It is a macabre journey replete with the reticulation of homosexuality, creativity, and death.

The Queen's astral body is entrusted symbolically to Doublemain, so named because his arms are articulated twice, his wrists serving as a second set of elbows. He transports his charge through glaucous marshland teeming with carnivorous insects resembling "horned feet." Such a stifling, green-tinted, fluid setting often indicates homosexual activity in Jarry's texts. Doublemain's back and face are green as well, like Haldern's skin when sexually stimulated. The implicit comparison of Doublemain to Haldern is sustained when Death's hideous envoy plunges his arms into the marsh to exhume a giant Hydrophilus, also referred to in the text wrongly but interestingly as a dung-beetle (912). The unorthodox symbolism of the hydrophilus marshals opulent comparisons.

Doublemain equates it to "the Book" and proceeds to unfold its wings in order to inscribe Salomon's name. In *Haldernablou* wings are most importantly identified with hands: the hands that stimulate sexually and that strangle. Comparable to the unbearable buzzing of the hydrophilus's wings—Doublemain has nailed it to the ferry mast and it struggles to be free—all sorts of grating and grinding sounds are associated with homosexual passion in *Haldernablou*. The effect of Ablou's hands on Haldern are further equated to that of the book *Les Chants de Maldoror* (226). Hands joined together as in prayer are analogous to the closing of a book (234). In the "Paralipomena" of *Haldernablou* the metaphor of the hands/book acquires phallic significance (237) in the context of *solitary* sexual pleasure, here too accompanied by "auditory apparitions" (238).

The suspicion that Jarry's consummate interest was self-love finds additional confirmation in "Adelphism and Nostalgia," the first chapter of "The Book of my Brother" (II) in *Days and Nights*. Sengle can no longer recall Valen's image and admits that "the Double is as empty and vain as a tomb" (768). He "discovers the real metaphysical cause of the happiness of loving: not the communion of two beings become one, like the two halves of man's heart, which is separately double in the foetus, but the pleasure of anachronism and chatting with one's own past (Valens undoubtedly loved his own future . . .)" (768). Sengle and Valens are the same person at two moments, two and half years apart, lived simultaneously. Sengle loves his own past, but being devoid of memory he needs a "living and visible friend" (769). In order to assure himself of their perfect match, Sengle leafs through a book, this time a book of heraldry, for their coats of arms, just as Doublemain "leafs through" Hydrophilus. The wings, hands, and book ultimately reveal the self and the double as identical, separated only by the time of memory. Homosexual passion thus is a literary conceit for intellectual masturbation.[26]

The monstrous insect also symbolizes the double in this role of creative auto-ejaculation by virtue of its equivalence to the brain, a dominant motif in Jarry's oeuvre and of utmost importance to Ubu's well-being. "Hydrophilus" describes a substance capable of absorbing water, in the manner of a sponge or gauze. Haldern imagines memory to be tangible and decides to kill Ablou in order to destroy all memory of his act, saying explicitly, "And I crush the brain like a sponge" (226). Brains are also likened to sponges absorbing water in "Opium": the setting is an immense morgue. By using memory creatively, these metaphors imply, one generates and masters oneself and one's world. Doublemain has, in fact, unearthed a giant, vitreous brain which holds the memory/water of the homosexually and morbidly charged marshland.

Doublemain realizes he has been duped (by Assaf) and begs Hydrophilus's pardon. He is horrified that he almost inscribed it with the name of the hideous, soulless being: that of a woman.[27] He frees Hydrophilus and, cursing women, shouts the name "Helen." Jarry's biographer, Noël Arnaud, suggests that Doublemain was invoking the gnostic Helen of whom Helen of Troy is but one incarnation. This supposition would be entirely consonant with Jarry's knowledge of occult traditions and the significance of the gnostic Helen meshes well with the major symbolism of the text.[28] Helen incarnates Thought, fallen and imprisoned in a human form by bad angels. Her male counterpart is the Spirit. She engenders all; he governs all. They are the two offshoots of Silence, an invisible, incomprehensible force. The being produced by their union, the Spirit inside Thought, is the hermaphrodite: this perfect symbol of doubling as a process of auto-projection—the process enacted by Jarry's heroes—depicts a being simultaneously single and double. Through the ages, Helen lived in various female forms. Her final incarnation was as the grand prostitute of Tyr. By making her his concubine, Simon the Magus concretely joined the Great Force—which he embodied—to Great Thought. In fact, in Samaria, the one God revered was the Androgyn, who became the Dea Deus of the occultists. Possession of Helen results in a union so complete that her lover becomes the male God within the female God.[29] It is not insignificant that Léon-Paul Fargue's nickname was "the Androgyn."

According to gnostic belief, Helen was to reappear in person on the seventh day of the seventh year of the restoration of the Gnosis: September 1896 to September 1897. By writing *The Other Alceste* on 23 August 1896, Jarry undoubtedly meant his drama as a portent of Helen's return the following week. The prophetic acumen of Doublemain's outburst is, however, coextensive with a virulent misogyny. He offers Queen Balkis to Hydrophilus whose nourishment consists of excrement; the insect disappears beneath the marsh kneading her in his paws. Doublemain waited but saw no sign of the bubble that indicates the soul's escape from the body. King Salomon himself asks God to foil his spouse's subterfuge since "a woman's soul must not be given in exchange for the soul of a prophet" (914).

In comparison to his disdain for women—before marrying Balkis he examined her in a room whose floor was inlaid with mirrors—the King admits a love for his son "that would be a sacrilege to prostitute on a woman" (914). The relationship between Salomon and Roboam parallels that of Sengle and Valens: the former sees his own past relived by the latter. It is Roboam who must, after all, sacrifice himself. Purity, while incompatible with heterosexuality, seems to be entirely reconcilable with homosexuality. Salomon instructs his son to eliminate Doublemain once he has been accepted as the King's substitute. A vicious duel ensues which leaves Roboam blind and Doublemain one-armed. The ferryman, doomed to row eternally in a circle, cannot fetch Salomon. This ensures the completion of the Temple and Salomon's personal immortality (unlike his Koranic model). His double, Roboam, likewise enters the realm of the eternal, for the loss of sight is often concomitant with the acquisition of "vision." The motif of blindness systematically informs Jarry's literary corpus. In *Haldernablou* the members of the Chorus knew their eyes would be torn out and Haldern has but to close his to enter eternity; while an owl plucks out Christ's eyes in *Caesar-Antichrist*. The motif also appears in *The Supermale*, "Au Paradis ou le Vieux de la Montagne" [In Paradise or The Old Man of the Mountain]; *Absolute Love*, and "Chez la Muse" [Visiting the Muse]. In *La Revanche de la Nuit* [The Revenge of Night] when owls' eyes are nailed shut (257) the birds become clairvoyant, suddenly familiar with eternity and Jarry's personal brand of homosexual "death." By barring the exterior world, the eye—a symbol of creativity—becomes an emblem of absolute inner genesis.

La Peur chez l'Amour [Fear Visiting Love]

This short piece, written entirely in dialogue, is the eighth of eleven vignettes that compose *Love Goes Visiting*, first published in May 1898. Like *The Other Alceste* it pits male against female to the detriment of the latter. A combination of the terrestrial and the astral, Love is infinitely more perspicacious than Fear who relies only on emotions. While instinctual Fear represents "eternally perfidious woman" (888), associated with negative and lunar forces, Love is male, envisioned positively as Apollo, bearer of oracles and of sunlight. Apollo, the patron of poets, is, significantly, the twin of Artemis, a virgin. Spiritual twinship is a capital theme of Jarry's opus.

Fear strives to consume Love in her passion: the double cannot consent to union. Symbolic walls rise abruptly to block Fear's vision; she sinks into mud. Clearsightedness cedes to infernal hallucinations in her quest to join Love:

> A new door. Oh! . . . This one is pretty. It is totally transparent, pale amethyst, rosy violet [. . .]. It is sealed with lead like a coffin. Behind it bodies of reptiles slide sluggishly about. Two white serpents [. . .]. These white serpents have suckers. They have tentacles. Long gossamer tentacles [. . .]. The new door that opens—shows me two arms, simply arms. . . . (885–86)

The spermous serpentine arms that reach out from this funereal domain belong to Love. In "Visions actuelles et futures" [Present and Future Visions], a text related to *Caesar-Antichrist,*[30] a comparison makes it clear that gossamer and sperm, like texturally similar brains, partake not only of the purity Jarry so coveted, but are even poetic entities (340).

The hermetically sealed chamber, a realm of purity and poetry, is Love's bedroom: sexuality becomes esoteric and arcane. While Love, however, prefers his "door to have no sexual opening," that is no keyhole, because it is "more chaste," he admits that at night "all doors are intoxicated, opened" (883). Nevertheless, Fear is not welcome at Love's house. She, like the reader, never finally enters the arcanum, but always faces some "wall," some sign at once a restraint and a lure.

Narcissistic and homosexual love again predominates. When Fear inquires, "Do you know yourself?" Love replies unequivocally, "With pleasure. I confess it . . . according to the temple of Apollo at Delphi" (886). Fear recognizes that "this room is sacred." It is a domain in which "one hears the spiders of one's brain spin their webs" (886). Gossamer spiders' webs, a frequent image in Jarry's texts, express the always-endangered purity of homosexual love. Haldern, for example, compares himself to a spider: he too completely governs his prey, imitating the cannibalistic spider, and spins a "web of silence" around Ablou (219), creating an abstract, dreamlike space comparable to Love's refuge.

Gaining access to that realm is synonymous with penetration into one's innermost self. The symbolism of both the serpent-arms and the spiral staircase leading to Love's room reinforce the mediation between two states of being as well as the danger of such an undertaking. Fear would like to be rid of her promiscuous life, symbolized by the dog who enters Love's house but does not join her in the dizzying climb toward chastity and death. Ascending the staircase represents plastically the "journey into oneself."[31]

Love's disconcerting mask and his highly condensed language emphasize his absolute purity. Like a surrealistic painting, his face becomes that of a clock: white, with three hands, of which the "first marks the hour, the second measures off the minutes, and the third, always immobile, eternalizes [his] indifference" (882). Equally inscrutable, Love's language contrasts sharply with Fear's excited verbosity. Fear recounts her search for God in whom she does not believe but whom she fears nonetheless. Love's hermetic retort, "Absurd. Absurd. Absolute. Absolute" (883) is interpretable only in the context of a statement made by the heroine of *The Supermale:* "I believe in it," she explains, speaking of absolute love, "because no one will believe in it . . . *because it is absurd . . .* just like I believe in God!"[32] Her belief in the absolute is due to the necessity that to believe in it requires a completely individual stand. Such an exceptional position is definitionally absurd since it has no links to the beliefs of others: it is absurd in the sense of being out of harmony. The quest for the absolute, a fundamental structure of Jarry's work, is coextensive with the quest for total individuality. The fact that Fear cannot breach the distance to Love—there is always an "inexplicable wall" forming the "angle of eternity" (887)—indicates that emotions (such as Fear) are the wrong route to take to purity. The conflict between these doubles continues to intensify as does their perverse separation. The longer Fear remains incapable of comprehending Love, the more imperious is her need to join him and the more frantic she becomes. Love maintains his lucid serenity, self-assurance, and his ability to appreciate the humorous aspects of life.

"Chez la Muse" [Visiting the Muse]

A lighthearted, slightly delirious combination of dialogue, prose, and poetry, this episode of *Love Goes Visiting* expatiates Jarry's profound interest in love, creation, and individuality. The antagonists reveal his ever-growing concern with abstraction. Here, they are not even named with impersonal designations such as Love or Fear. "Him" and "Her" argue over whether the latter, the Muse, ought to permit the former, the poet, to enter her abode.

"Visiting the Muse" opens with a semi-comical, pastoral ditty which, with one reprise, will also close the piece, but the first speech by Him sets the stage for serious preoccupations. He refers to his footsteps as "deserters of the beaten path" (888), establishing his similarity to Sengle. His tracks, covered by a rain of ashes, have led him to the closed door of Her, the unknown beauty. Similar to Love's door, this one has both sexual and menacing features. It is depicted as a target that must be attacked. The keyhole is likened to a wound which, in *The Other Alceste,* described the female genital. The assault must thus be sexual in nature. Enemy territory glimpsed by the suitor through the pierced flesh of the precious door resembles a cemetery. An owl cries among the dead women in it, introducing the homosexual overtones (connoted by the owl) of this relationship ostensibly uniting a male and female. In "Prolegomena of Haldernablou," for example, in the context of a homosexual encounter between Vulpian and Aster, the male genital is as "beautiful as an owl hung by its claws" (212).

Rejected, the poet wanders off into the prairie where his monologue definitively evinces the theme of homosexuality. He claims he would have preferred "the right road, entirely unified" (890), but that everything was ruined by the rain of ashes. Like falling black sand in *Les Minutes de sable mémorial,* falling rain showers or tempests, especially of ashes (but also, elsewhere, of sulpher and asphalt) strongly connote homosexual activity. The poem "Le Sablier" [The Hourglass], part of *Les Minutes,* establishes the metaphorical equivalence of the space between the earth and the sky and the skull's interior, which also signifies Haldern's fateful room. The storms that occur in this space signify the intense inner emotions of pederastic excitement. Two poems in "The Revenge of Night" purposefully entitled "Rain of War" and "Rain of Hunting" methodically elaborate homosexual imagery. The road the poet has followed—in addition to being the site of the ashen rainfall—is, moreover, not the unified path he would have chosen but is a divided one: that of the deserter, that is the double.

Furthermore, the poet announces the need to invent new rhythms. The passage from the old to the new order occasions the falling of the stars from the sky. This fall recurrently indicates the apocalyptic death of the outer world necessarily following homosexual pleasure. It corresponds to the shutting of the eyes, but whereas one controls one's own eyelids, God commands the stars. In *Les Minutes* their fall manifests punishment by God. Here, it is the violence of the poet's sneezes that will precipitate the fall. Not only is the sneeze ejaculatory in nature, but the poet clearly assumes a divine role, majestically addressing his fellowmen as "little earthlings" (891). In "Present and Future Visions" a speech addressed to the phallic *bâton-à-physique* graphically characterizes stars as "the cerebral rice of your pearly sperm" (340).

After his second sneeze, the poet compares the stars, with their rays, to green spines of chestnuts that can get in one's eyes.[33] Green, as it does in *The Other Alceste* (especially in the imagery of the marshland) symbolizes sexual activity, creativity, and morbidity. The association with the dangerous and phallic spiny protrusions of the chestnuts reinforces the symbolism. These spines are subsequently metaphorized to the poet's own eyelashes. He decides to close his eyes: his lashes will cause the apocalyptic starless sky, which is thus the inner space behind the poet's eyelids. The fact that eyelashes are described as a "mask" in *Absolute Love* (952) underscores the autocreative aspects of "possession" by the double.[34] If the stars are equivalent to sperm, and their points to eyelashes, and the closing of the eyelashes (also parallel to a violent sneeze) causes the stars to fall, then the seminal movement is evidently an autoerotic one. Ejaculation is self-induced; insemination is inner-directed and cerebral, occurring behind closed eyes.

Immediately following the telling decision to close his eyes, the spurned poet falls asleep. Only then does the Muse open her door: her appearance recalls the hallucinations of the "Propos des Assassins." Indeed, the poet of *Love Goes Visiting* overtly compares himself to Sengle when he counsels "Let's try not to fly back overseas!" (890), alluding to the scene in which Sengle fears his head will permanently detach itself from his body. There is a footnote in "Visiting the Muse" referring the reader to *Days and Nights, Novel of a Deserter*. Sengle's metaphor for madness certainly seems apt, given the description of the Muse who stands naked on her threshold. Covering "the triangle of her sex" a triangular chastity belt embossed with pearls emits electrical rays. *Les Minutes* offer an explanation of the triangle's symbolism. The doubled triangular structure of the hourglass projects a "three-cornered hat" onto the sky—the sky becomes the hat—and a "triangular forest" onto the ground, this last the setting for *Haldernablou*. It is between the two projections that the storms indicative of extremely powerful inner sexual turmoil occur. Electrical impulses—the lightning of the storm—manifest the heightened excitation of nerves. Enclosure in the triangular space exposes one to the temporal effects of the hourglass's falling sand, another metaphor for falling (homosexual) rain. Triangulation, flowing sand/time, and pederasty are also linked in "The Revenge of Night": "Le temps vanne mes Heures de son pentagonal écusson noir, pelle enfoncé dont le Triangle émerge" (249).[35]

The description of the Muse further specifies that her hermetically sealed blind eyes are those of a chameleon. In the first of *Haldernablou's* Prolegomena the chameleon's eyes are likened to God's sacred Phallus (212). Jarry's introductory woodcut depicts Haldern and Ablou in profile, face to face, beneath a chameleon whose eyes translate the disquiet of a sexual encounter. Jarry carefully points out that the Muse's chameleonlike eyes are "independent," that is each constantly moves—and in all directions—independently from the other. The squinting and contorting of the eyes that result illustrates the effects on the victim of sexual aggression. In the "Heraldic Act" of *Caesar-Antichrist* we learn that Caesar-Antichrist and the chameleon are one and the same (287): throughout this Act the joining of dormant matter to a creative intellect becomes a prolonged metaphor of pederasty. The Muse's companions, bats and owls with phosphorescent claws, complete the symbolism of the paradoxically fatal but creative homosexual experience.

Suddenly, in excactly the same manner as did Haldern and Ablou, the poet and the Muse exchange roles: he becomes sadistic, calling her a sorceress and commanding her to kneel before him. Love is always associated with aggression; it must be stimulated in the love object by the superior partner. Finally, he, in turn, banishes the Muse because she could offer him only pleasures of the flesh and was incapable of awakening his profound inner self. She kneels, sharing his fate.

His dying words accuse death of being plagiarism. Clearly, the "death" that is the outcome of the poet's adventure, like the "deaths" of Sengle and other "deserters" must be interpreted as a literary conceit for the substitution of words from outside one's subjectivity for those we possess. For Jarry, this is tantamount to forfeiting our brain cells and accepting replacements from the exterior. *Décervelage* is not simply the business of Ubu on the rampage. It is a metaphor for one of Jarry's most serious concerns. The disembraining or "plagiarism" that interested him was neither the unquestioning assimilation of ideas forced upon one nor the monitoring of one's thoughts in any way. His conception of an intentionally and freely chosen "exchange of brain cells" allowed for the acquisition of new ideas only by displacement. "Death," then, is infinitely creative. To claim, as does the poet, that "death is not eternal" (893) affirms its dynamic nature.

Au Paradis ou le Vieux de la Montagne [In Paradise or The Old Man of the Mountain]

In conjunction with "Fear Visiting Love" and "Visiting the Muse," within the larger context of *Love Goes Visiting* this short five-act play delineates the gap between impure corporeal passions and spiritual, absolute love. It links the dominant motifs of sexuality, aggression, and murder. The visit to the Old Man of the Mountain becomes a sojourn in the paradise inhabited by the double. Continuing the search for a terrestrial paradise—the prolonged "real hallucination" (*Days and Nights,* 794)—Marc-Pol and Cinghis-Khan are initiated into the world of mystical reality by drinking the halluncinatory brew of the Prophet, chief of the Hassassins, whose followers are simultaneously assassins and users of hashish. In the subsequent narcotic dreams day can no longer be distinguished from night: this metaphor encodes the passage from the physical to the pataphysical. Logic and time surrender to a perpetual regeneration made possible by human blood and semen. The transcendence offered by the double is entirely human, attainable by achieving a certain state of consciousness. Desire may be fulfilled, pataphysically, in an irrational space.

The spatialization into Paradise of spiritual purity creates the décor of this drama, a walled mountain chateau which provides the sole passage to the edenic valley. Like the staircase to Love's chamber, the mountain symbolizes the desire to escape to another—unsullied and sanctified—dimension. Because of its verticality, the mountain is phallic and uranic. This vertical scenic structure, which corresponds to the play's psychological configuration, is further reinforced by the potent symbol of Marc-Pol's sword. The weapon betokens virility and purity, sublimation and spiritualization. In its vertical position it impales the head of the hero's adversary: this scene, emblematic of the double, evokes both Ubu's atrocities and Sengle's fateful promenade with Valens during which he expresses his fear of madness, or figurative decapitation.

Marc-Pol's entry into paradise is fraught with paradox. The Scheik offers him the Princess's hand and places his golden necklace around the young man's neck. It transmutes into a noose when he is lifted into the air, thus becoming isomorphic with a bird, itself a symbol of the sublimation of Eros. As he strangles, Marc-Pol believes himself to be in the arms of his bride. His ejaculation, his entry into paradise, and his death are concomitant. Indeed, virility presupposes chastity, and destruction proves seminal.

Strangulation, especially by hanging, appertains to one of Jarry's chief sexual obsessions. In *Absolute Love,* he proclaims "hanging is the Youth of the Old Man" (956). Dr. Faustroll, in fact, hangs himself in an autoerotic episode from which he recovers spontaneously (659). For Jarry, suffocation, be it from hanging, drowning, or other methods, connotes sexual climax. Speaking of hanging in an article in *La Revue Blanche,* he called it a sport akin—owing to the simultaneity of being "executor" and "patient"—to masturbation.[36]

The canon governing sexual symbolism becomes explicit by means of intertextual readings. Diurnal and nocturnal differentiation depends upon two beacons of light, called *obéliscolychnies* in the text, a rarely used term nevertheless employed three times in this short drama. The word refers the reader to "Amber," the prose piece in *Days and Nights* that recounts a tale of Sapphic twinship. Thus, although a heterosexual marriage furnishes the plot, the psychosemiotic plane provides the deeper meaning of homosexual love. "Amber"—the story of lesbian sisters—actually mirrors the relationship of Sengle and Valens. The *obéliscolychnie* recalls the "masts of men's ships" (790). This sign of male sexuality is directly linked to the word "amber" by Marc-Pol: "I have your golden necklace and your arms of white amber around my neck like the rays of the sun and the moon on the two *obéliscolychnies*" (900). Elsewhere in the text, the sun produces its rays when it "ejaculates golden pollen" (896). It follows that Marc-Pol strangles because of sexual paroxysm and not—as physiology would have it—vice versa. In order to enter paradise, in which day and night remain indistinguishable, sexual activity—symbolized by the pair of light beacons, the sun rays, and the silvery ashes pouring from the moon (equivalent to the ashen rain and the falling black sand of *Les Minutes de sable mémorial*)—must be surpassed.

It is highly significant that Jarry once again chose the Hassassins to people his drama. In exchange for initiation and the right to partake of the potion—whence the passage into paradise—the Hassassin is obliged to commit homicide, or as in the case of Sengle, fratricide. Given the role of the double, such fratricide constitutes a variation of suicide. Metaphorically, one lives one's own death for the duration of the séance. Suicide, moreover, frequently provides the most desirable route to the supplementary universe. For one thing, it indemnifies perfect egotism, and represents the individual's absolute control of his own life and death. Thus, the apparent motifs of sexuality, aggression, and murder, channeled further—on the level of connotation—to homosexuality, sadism, and fratricide, refer ultimately to climactic autoeroticism, ritualized sadomasochism, and glorious suicide: double or nothing.

Chapter Five

Love

L'Amour absolu [Absolute Love]

Tragic and condemned, Oedipal love provides the route to absolute love and to the pure realm of thought. Emmanuel God, half-man–half-God, interacts with permutations of the maternal archetype. Obsessed with the purity of love, this son struggles to rejoin the female who engendered him, at once virgin and mother, mistress and wife, lover and Siren. Emulating his jarryan avatars, Emmanuel God belongs to that tribe of "great criminals" (923), the possessed murderers who pioneer the unknown.

The novel opens with Emmanuel God imprisoned and condemned to death. He awaits the "sidereal hour" when his "head will take leave" (921). These two clues—astral time and decapitation—indicate the metaphorical essence of Emmanuel God's sentence, and inscribe him in the genealogy of Haldern, Sengle, and Marc-Pol. More explicitly, "he has no other prison but the cranial box, and is but a man who dreams, seated near his lamp" (921). Only at the novel's end do we learn the crime: matricide. Emmanuel God murdered Varia (Mary in the Breton language), the terrestrial form of the Virgin, in order to rejoin Miriam (the Aramaic equivalent of Mary), the "true" Virgin. There is no doubt that the Passion recounted concerns the God of the supplementary universe.

The detached head indicates a gap between identity and desire. Intricate and subtle, the symbolism of the liberated head recuperates elements in the complex interrelationships between Emmanuel God and eternal femininity. Its equation to a prison, an eye, and a lamp circumscribes an enclosed dramatic space. Like Ubu inside the Gidouille and Sengle in his barracks, or in the hospital, Emmanuel God exists within an irrational and symbolic space demarcated textually by "skulls," "attics," "vaults," and "caves." These special sites have a common denominator: somber and dangerous interiority.

The image of the snail channels Emmanuel God's excessive and incongruous impulses into the realm of absolute femininity, a point between the separable identities of the objects of his affection and hatred. Entering the spiral-shelled snail (921) guarantees the ontological stability of a synthetic and hermetic universe; life within recreates the protective calm of uterine enclosure. The snail represents perfect aquatic femininity and, thus, permanence amid the fluctuations of time. Absolute love goes hand in hand with desire for immortality. Sea and moon, both ancient symbols of femininity, combine to signify the eternal: in this case, the lunar world of sleep. Sleep, parallel to the somnolent and fluid fetal environment inside the Mother, functions as "provisional eternity" (920), since it "apes death" (924).

Exhibiting an instinctual need for the sea, Emmanuel God peers through the windows of the Saint-Lazare train station which resembles an aquarium. The train (or locomotive), like Sengle's "lunar train," facilitates the commutation to the supplementary universe, imagined here as the domestication of the primeval waters. As his mother (having come by train to visit during his school vacation) approaches him, lifting the "door curtain of fluid crystal" he cannot believe the woman is his mother: "she was coming toward him too much like a siren" (938).

This threatening, seductive, and fatal aspect of the female correlates as well to the repeated image of the octopus or devil-fish. Maternal arms metamorphose into tentacles that "explore" Emmanuel God's body, confirming the transformation of his mother, Madame Joseb, wife of the notary, into Varia, wife of the Biblical carpenter. As the danger intensifies, images focus on sadistic devouring by a sharp-fanged wolf. The tables are turned, however, when Emmanuel God asserts his extraordinary powers to subjugate the sorceress to his will. Varia subsequently awakens from a nightmarish chase only to rediscover two black wolves "under Emmanuel's two eyebrows" (937). The aggression he vents on this "enemy" (his double: he and Varia are literally the same size) is the same as the aggression this hostile mother made him endure.

Love—as Haldern made clear to Ablou—demands absolute submission; Emmanuel God controls Varia with his eyes/wolves. A dark liquid flows from his pupils into Varia's, materializing "the dregs of Love which is Fear" (943), a definition equally pertinent to "Fear Visiting Love." These savage eyes are emblematic of his identity: "Monsieur God's eyes are an ornament of his costume, even when he is entirely naked" (949). Endowed with their formidable powers of domination and enthrallment, if shut to the exterior world eyes act as "doors of the flesh that open onto Truth" (949). When "eyelashes intersect" they "brutally poke the hearth of absolute love" (951). Thus, absolute love or Truth hides behind closed eyes and demands active and probably painful stimulation before it "ignites."

A curious sodality, the trio Mme Joseb, Varia, and Miriam replace one another by a process of "absorption" or "drinking" accomplished by the eye: "Miriam, in order *to be,* annihilated Varia: the blond eyes of the Wife of God, like a mouth, grazed the black eyelashes and the eyebrows of Mme Joseb, and drank as far as the vague violet of her tresses. It is by an analogous absorption that Mme Joseb substituted her whole being for Miriam" (951). The erotogenicity of the eye has replaced normal sexual activity. A pataphysically erogenous zone, the eye is perfectly androgynous: absorptive and penetrating (compared to "bayonettes" and "pokers"). When closed, it is absolutely creative within the limits of the "cranial box," a prison—reminiscent of that in *Ubu Enchained*—with boundless potential.

Doors to inner Truth, closed eyes permit Emmanuel God to create his own absolute love, that is to give form to his desire. Miriam

records the Truth he improvises. She is, at his will, absolute Truth. Human Truth, it is what man wants:
    a *desire.*
The Truth of God, what he *creates.*
When one is neither one nor the other—Emmanuel—, *his* Truth, it is the *creation of his desire.* (950)

And Miriam, in a hypnotic sleep, claims to be the "Will of God" (925). The attainment of this state once again resembles death; Miriam, in her perfection, resembles an inert statue (946). In order to assure the longevity of his pure creation, Emmanuel God decides he must murder Varia, certain that this act would in no way jeopardize Miriam, who is entirely external to her negative counterpart (957). As André Green observes in *The Tragic Effect,* however, by choosing to love the woman most unlike his mother—"not other than his mother, but exactly the converse"— he unknowingly "falls back" on "the Same, the inevitable Mother."[1]

He arrogantly attempts to join his perfect creation, and—a compelling echo of Sengle—"loses his head," symbolized here too by a kite (958). Reciprocally, then, the inevitable outcome of his incestuous love ("I am the Son, I am your son, I am the Spirit, I am your husband for all eternity, your husband and your son, very pure Jocasta!" [p. 925]) plunges the son into eternal darkness. Through death, though, the inner-directed eye becomes clairvoyant. In *Caesar-Antichrist* Jarry had already expressed his conception of death as the "concentrated reapprehending of Thought: it no longer radiates infinitely toward the exterior world; its circumference, nyctalopic pupil, retracts toward its center; it is thus that it becomes God, that it begins to be" (281). For implicit in the quest for absolute love is the theory of being fashioned in *To Be and To Live.* To accede to the world of pure ideas requires not action, living, and expansion, but infinite condensation and synthesis (923) (iconized by the nyctalopic pupil) accomplished in isolation by the individual. Emmanuel God undertakes the timeless project by exercising his memory, the ultimate "time machine." Retracting his being totally into memories of his childhood, and viewing his past with the "mind's eye," as it were, he reconstitutes the perfect generative matrix, the True Virgin-Mother.

Although Emmanuel God desires his mother, apostrophized as Jocasta, he does not commit parricide, but accomplishes the oedipal tragedy in its negative phase, that is to say, matricide. Another facet of the oedipal complex reveals the desirer killing the object of desire. The hero of mythology Emmanuel most resembles is Orestes,[2] for the dagger Orestes plunges into his mother's breast is likewise Emmanuel God's weapon; and both act in full consciousness. Although the murders themselves are lucidly committed, *Absolute Love,* like the *Oresteia,* is "imbued with the power of darkness," unfolding in the dimension of the nightmare.[3] The novel opens with "Let there be darkness!", the apocalyptic title of the first chapter. Mythology and legends illustrate a causal relationship between matricide and the dark night of madness.

Absolute Love begins and also ends with references to darkness, death, serpents (worms, snakes, reptiles), and eroticism. Night, abruptly ushered in when the novel begins, sets the scene for Emmanuel God's imprisonment in death row. We soon learn that one change brought by nightfall is the transformation of cyclists and coachmen into desiring female glowworms. Emmanuel God's crime and madness, associated from the beginning with the image of the amorous female worm, thus pertain to the psychological figure of phallic mother, who takes over the paternal potency and becomes the possessor of phallic power.[4] The father's presence is superfluous and his speech is not revered. He is neither the object of the mother's desire nor "the sign by which the phallus enters the child's world through the discovery of its absence at the level of the mother."[5]

Emmanuel God's father is first mentioned in a chapter whose epigraph, "to find out that one's mother is a virgin," denies this female's sexual relationship with her husband. In the course of the ensuing dialogue between the newborn son and his virgin mother (addressed as Jocasta and "my little wife"), the child declares that his mother's virginity assures his divinity. The cradle is assimilated to the nuptial bed. The mother's sexuality is thus reserved exclusively for this male infant, a fact emphasized by the activity of the father: a carpenter, he is whittling, generating wood shavings shaped like little horns, symbols of the cuckold. The verb *faire germer* ("to cause to germinate") joined with *cornes* ("horns") implies that the only thing disseminated and engendered by the aged father is his own lack of sexuality.

The parallel between the phallic mother and Emmanuel's is further established by the absorptive relationship between Varia and Miriam. While in Orestes' case his mother Clytemnestra sent the Erinyes "to empty Orestes by absorption of the substance with which his body is filled," the process (if not the substance transferred) is identical to that functioning in *Absolute Love*; the passage (by absorption) of the existence of one being into the other in Jarry's novel occurs because of Emmanuel's desire. He is intimately implicated in the "vampire-like relation that marks the relations between the image of the phallic mother [Clytemnestra] and the fruit of her womb."[6]

The mythic Erinyes, by virtue of having snakes for hair, also bring the psychological dynamics of castration into play. As Freud remarked of Medusa's head, the multiple phallic symbols (the snakes) serve to deny castration. The snake-as-hair substitutes for the nonexistent penis in the female, and it is this absence (in the female genitals) which provokes horror.[7] This image of castration—the female with snakes instead of hair—is faced by Orestes and by Emmanuel after their symbolic castration of the mother. Both also confront the Python, a monstrous chtonian, and maternal, serpent that crushes its prey. Orestes killed the Python and had to be cleansed of this crime; Emmanuel, similarly, prays to the Virgin Mary after the appearance of the Python, who is compared in the text to vipers (venomous snakes). Echidna, the monstrous viper of mythology, half-woman, half-snake, joined incestuously with her son Orthrus to produce the Sphinx, the figure par excellence of the phallic mother.

The seductive phallic mother further appears as the snake in the form of Melusina, a devouring Siren with a serpent's tail. The text significantly identifies this mermaid (whose name is thrice mentioned in *Absolute Love*, aside from figuring in a chapter title) with a flying kite, alluding to the kite/head in *Days and Nights* that risks flying away. Decapitation and Melusina are again conflated by the allusion of the title of chapter 13 ("Melusina Was a Scullery Maid, Pertinax a Nut Sheller") to chapter 30 in Rabelais's *Pantagruel* ("How Epistemon, Who Had His Head Cut Off, Was Ably Cured by Panurge and Some News of Devils and Damned"). In this chapter, Rabelais lists the fates chosen for many famous people damned to Hell, among them Melusina and Pertinax, whose sentences are reiterated in Jarry's title. Rabelais's title further contains a spoonerism pertinent to the symbolism of Melusina in Jarry's text: Rabelais's *la couppe testée* offers Jarry the possibility of a play on "head" and "testes," decapitation and castration. In a final reference near the novel's end, the name "Melusina" appears alone on a line of textual space otherwise blank save for three eliptical dots following the name. Emmanuel God's Oedipal dilemma, it would seem, is not merely a lure into some void, is not an unreachable signified, a kite flying into and leaving behind nothingness. This absence, implied and imprinted, must be interpreted as the collective detours and tracks traced in relation to the absent signified: Oedipal complex.

Immediately following "Melusina . . ." the text continues, "Upon a sudden rain, as is frequent in Lampaul—and it was quite necessary that THE OTHER God cry, since Emmanuel did not have the desire to *himself,* the wind ceased" (Jarry's emphases; 958). The threads of significance converging in this event are entangled in the problematics of the Other. First, the absorptive process of exchange between doubles (Varia and Miriam) occurs in the "Melusina" chapter (13). Second, that chapter's epigraph ("INTERMISSION: The stars fall from the sky") separates the "Acte Prologal" from the "Acte Héraldique" in *Caesar-Antichrist.* This coming of darkest night symbolizes, in Jarry's imagery, death which must follow union in passion with one's double. The vampirization by the double is thus connected with the death of Christ and the (re)birth of Caesar-Antichrist, whose reign the "Heraldic Act" identifies with the sadistic connotations of the blazon Orle. Thus are linked decapitation, castration, damnation, and vampirization and all are subsumed by the emergence of the Other, imagined here as Melusina, an avatar of the Python, Echidna, and the Sphinx. This last, called "the divine double of

Oedipus, whose nature [like Emmanuel God's] is both divine and human,"[8] symbolizes incest, the psychological equivalent of matricide.

"THE OTHER God" who must cry because Emmanuel would not, is Emmanuel God's double, the phallic mother: "He is the same size as Varia. [. . .] The breasts of one [hers] are the exact copy of the breasts of the other. They are two exactly super-imposable triangles. [. . .] They turn aside like a book opens" (942–43). In the important scene where the divine male infant seduces his virginal mother, she offers to kill her husband if her son so commands, clearly taking on the potent role. The father's impotence is coextensive with his exclusion from the literacy of the other two (they are like a "book") and from their discourse. He neither speaks to them nor hears them: "And all that is said, Joseph does not hear it, because it is necessary that he not hear it." The uncertainty of the word *entendre* is in play, for it means both "to hear" and "to understand" (924). Excluded from discourse, he is excluded from signification, play and power. He is described, lest there be any doubt, as "writing and reading hardly at all" (929).

The Other, then, emerges as the locus of perception and of signification, and as proprietress of the signified, much like the Sphinx possesses the totality of meaning while Oedipus, who finally answers the Sphinx's riddle, is still propelled by a desire and an inability to know. Emmanuel God, at the mercy of the viper, is condemned to the torment of desire leading to self-destruction. His punishment for transgression of a taboo, like that inflicted on Aeschylus's Orestes, is to be subjected to the "human court of the city."[9] Emmanuel God's passage takes him across a carpet of reptiles and into a prison called *La Santé: la santé* means "health" but a *maison de santé* means "mental hospital." This *"prison de LA SANTE"* represents civil justice but also judgment by the superego, symbolized by the prison's resemblance to "Argus who had one hundred eyes." Of this hundred, half remained always opened, whence his symbolic function of clairvoyance and surveillance. A harsh sentence awaits the anti-hero on both fronts: "Emmanuel God awaits the sidereal hour so his head may take leave" (921).

Le Surmâle {The Supermale}

Unique among Jarry's novels, *The Supermale*—while exhibiting the disconnection of poetic imagery—does exhibit a discernible plot. The protagonist, a mild-mannered, debonair fellow, undergoes two major metamorphoses (thanks to costumes) which call into question his true identity. First, he becomes "Le Pédard," an Olympian cyclist who rivals a locomotive in a spectacular race; second, he assumes the role—or is this the real man?—of "L'Indien" in the climactic scene where he makes good an earlier boast à propos of love-making. A tragic anti-climax pits the Supermale against the Love-Inspiring-Machine which sinks its white-hot teeth into all too mortal flesh.

André Marcueil, a sexual champion obsessed by corporeal mastery, embodies the quest for absolute virility. Clues to his Dionysian undertaking appear in the novel's first scene, a dinner at Marcueil's mansion. Difficult as it is for his guests to believe the utterance, Marcueil pronounces the prophetic words that open *The Supermale,* slyly subtitled "modern novel": "Making love is an act without importance, since one can do it indefinitely."[10] Although the evening's conversation addresses the topic of love (in order not to bore the ladies with talk of business), Marcueil's statement shocked the others. To judge by appearances, Marcueil's pallid, weak, and ailing body surely precluded any sex life.

By means of a language that intends more than it says, Jarry wastes no ink concealing Marcueil's true nature from the reader. In a manner structurally similar to Faustroll's odyssey, Marcueil stalks the absolute through infinite repetition, and in that sense the Supermale functions in physically oriented counterpoint to the cerebral Docteur. To those versed in Jarry's symbolism, the encrypted scene offers two further clues to our valetudinarian hero's "other" self. First, Marcueil sports golden spectacles with smoked-glass lenses which prevent a precise identification of his eye color. Since eyes symbolize the doors to the Truth, and to the inner self, the fact that Marcueil's are secreted behind a smoke-screen indicates that the dinner host's appearance disguises an identity too powerful and/or dangerous to circulate in public. The second clue to Marcueil's spurious normality situates the reader outside of clock-time: the château's clock, inexplicably destroyed, spilled its works onto the floor "like the entrails of a beast, the face grimaced and its hand madly turned two or three times like a trapped being seeking a way out" (129). Marcueil's home obviously delimits a supplementary universe, beyond conventional chronology.

In a seemly fashion, Ellen Elson stood apart from the discussion of sexual prowess. It is therefore all the more surprising that this chaste young girl be the sole person to comprehend the exceptional significance of Marcueil's speech recounting the amorous exploits of the Indian of Theophrastes (aided by a certain herb—Jarry's *herbe sainte,* absinthe?): "The virgin gazed directly into the pupilless gaze of the lorgnon:—I believe in the Indian, she murmured" (131). The sharing of this secret, a sort of password, relates to sexual familiarity and sexual knowledge. Throughout the novel, Ellen appreciates Marcueil's singularity and remarkable anatomy, and is the only one to recognize him beneath all of his disguises. She will become his partner in a pataphysical experiment to surpass the borders of the possible by means of the act of love.

Ellen's second entrance defines her role as Marcueil's double. She arrives "piloting" a car which speeds toward the château's front steps like a monstrous winged horse and signals its aggressive approach by a siren. A play on words transfers to Ellen the attributes of a Siren, a treacherous and supernatural female. Now wearing a shaggy pink driver's mask, she sees through the sham of Marcueil's monk's robe and whispers the password to her fellow "deserter": "The Indian so honored by Theophrastes" (151–52). The Supermale's equal but opposite, she incarnates the Superfemale, his condign counterpart, the absolute Woman, compared in the text to the women in *Absolute Love.* Ellen is multiple: virgin and sorceress. The conversation during this unexpected visit—Marcueil caught without his glasses and forced to lower his eyes—lends credence to the events that follow. Ellen posits the existence of an absolute Lover because woman imagines him and compares this to the proof of the soul's immortality: "human beings, owing to fear of nothingness, aspire to it." She believes in this Lover as she believes in God, "because it is absurd," because "no one will believe in him" (54). By imagining an impossible lover she satisfies her paradoxical desire for both sensual pleasure and virginity. Marcueil's indecorous speculation on the Indian-as-Lover describes the moment just before taking leave of human strength: "beyond . . . ELEVEN [. . .] the pleasure must be about the same as that felt by the teeth of a saw ground by a file" (55).

Miss Elson strategically regains the purity of her role as spectator during the race between a locomotive and a five-man cycle whose riders are nourished by Perpetual-Motion-Food (a concoction of alchohol and strychnine) to which they owe their exceptional endurance. Without the supplementary diet, Marcueil, first perceived as an uncanny Shadow and newly disguised in what appears to be a frock-coat and top hat, handily beats the team.[11] Only Ellen, gazing with love from a locomotive window, recognizes the fantastic racer who hastily disappears.

Marcueil and Ellen meet again at the château to embark on a project as absolute Lovers. Their perfect symmetry—"they were so absolutely the same size" (197)—reveals the facticious nature of the Indian's sadism; in Jungian terms, they represent the animus and the anima of one person. In fact, in the scene where Marcueil's eyes are unshielded, Ellen intuits, "I read in your eyes, your eyes that I see entirely naked today, that if one must believe in metempsychosis, you were, in some ancient time, a very old courtesan." Indeed, Ellen replaces the seven courtesans convoked to serve as a foil to the Indian's stamina, but relegated to the function of spectators. She embodies the projection of Marcueil's anima, his feminine psychological component. The Indian's explicit sadism manifests the painful and violent essence of the sexual encounter but it is actually an instance of sado-masochism. In his article "Battre les femmes" [To Beat Women] Jarry defined "the work of the flesh" as an "interior castigation."[12] Here, as elsewhere, sexuality portends death. Sexual knowledge is a figure of death, of ultimate absence. The inevitability of this association is foreshadowed by a fatal rape on the château grounds, most likely committed by Marcueil, of a girl who "died in a hardly usual fashion: she was not raped first and assassinated afterward, as is admissable; but . . . how to put it? *raped to death*" (179). It is interesting to note that "Indian" is the name given to Jarry by the housekeeper at the Phalanstère.

Sadistic, mechanical, painful, and fatal: love, for the Supermale, is an act, not a sentiment. Ellen, however, conceives a plan destined to make Marcueil fall in love with her. An electrical machine is built—the text fetishizes the machine, in the forms of a strength-testing device, a car, a locomotive, a cycle, a phonograph, and finally a robot—in order to "inspire" love in Marcueil. But man's potential exceeds that of any machine and the Supermale inspires love in the Machine who unexpectedly falls in love with *him*. Tragically, the current reverses: it electrifies the metal crown on Marcueil's head (he had ironically prophesied to Ellen: "all courtesans are queens" [p. 154]) which becomes an "incandescent jaw." This boomerang effect of the electrical circuit reinforces the structurally sado-masochistic love of the Supermale for Ellen. His horrible death, patently self-inflicted, offers the only absolute possible: death through love. The significance of the machine's grotesque "biting" of the Indian becomes clear in *Love Goes Visiting* when Lucien teaches his fiancée that "the bite is the sex act in a heightened state."[13]

But once again, given the essential structure of Jarry's creation, that is the protagonist's projection of a textual double, the "bite" must be self-directed, like the reverse current of the machine which returns toward Marcueil's head. A remark made by one of the guests during the opening conversation on love foreshadows this final scene. Bathybius tells of an epileptic idiot who gave his whole life "almost without interruption to sexual acts. But . . . in solitary, which explains a lot." He explained to the horrified women present that he meant "cerebral excitation explains everything" (19). Thus, the blissful, fatal passage to the absolute requires acute mental orgasm.

Messaline, roman de l'ancienne Rome
[Messalina, Novel of Ancient Rome]

This work is a prime example of the idiosyncratic rendering of history and mythology illustrated in *The Other Alceste*. There, Jarry attends to the Grecian Helen who reappears in *The Supermale* as Ellen's underlying identity, a consubstantiality mirrored by the sound of their names: Ellen/Hélène. The complex intersection of naming and being characteristic of these texts also underpins the Roman Empress's universe.

Messalina (A.D. 15–48), third wife of Claudius I, mother of Britannicus and Octavia, was a renowned debaucheress. Under Jarry's pen, she rivals Marcueil in libido. A novel also fetishizing the body-as-machine and the split personality, *Messaline* is a pendant to *The Supermale*. Here, the heroine incarnates all that is female and feminine: the goddess Acca Larentia, Venus, the Roman she-wolf, the city, the night. Empress and prostitute, the emblem of her house—the house of Happiness—portrays a large Phallus carved in the wood of a fig tree. It symbolizes universal life, the generative god. Since the front door is likened to a vulva, the house must itself be a large womb. Behind each interior partition, another perversion enacts every sexual obsession. Messalina becomes inextricably entangled in her labyrinthian search for Love, for the God of Love. In a surrealistic sequence she comprehends that she must descend toward the mysterious depths of the God's temple. Alas, the God she discovers loves but his own body. Messalina, in fact, flees at the dreadful weight and brutality of the presence of the sacred Phallus in her hands.

A potion, sardonically named "absinthe" will, she hopes, surely cause the God of Love to fall irresistibly in love with her. Unsuccessful, Messalina cedes to the temptation of possessing many men rather than one god. She abruptly regains her imperial demeanor, however, upon accepting the gift of a sword from her mother. The object replaces all men. In her ecstasy, she impales herself on the monstrous steel god. This gruesome sexual apotheosis dramatically utilizes the symbolism of the sword's deadly "bite," the same one the machine inflicted on Marcueil. Messalina, in the course of her ecstatic suicide, realizes that "one can only die of love."[14]

She could only travel beyond the "limits" of human capability by an act of individual volition. By consciously giving herself to the metal phallus, this superfemale deifies the obscene, and this in the etymological sense as well: glorification of the exoscenic. The sterility of her promiscuity maintains her virginal aura. It is precisely the nonreciprocity of her relationships that affords this female Don Juan her escape to the realm of the absolute, symbolized by precious stones as well as the cold metallic force of the sword itself.

The mechanical automatism with which she pursues Love, similar to the repetition of the same gesture by Marcueil, finally leads to the perfection of (metaphorical) suicide, representing absolute control of one's individuality. In combat against their own human limits, Messalina and Marcueil, literary twins, play at Love as if it were the most marvelous game or sport. As such, Love appears in all its ritualistic splendor. The game of love, concretized in the Phallus itself in *Messalina,* and generalized to instinctual man (the Indian) in *The Supermale,* leads to an erotic absolute, rather than to a love providing hope of transcendence. Indeed, Love itself must be conquered in the process of this game which, like Pataphysics, is a means of imaginary solutions. The elusive Phallus submits to possession only in exchange for the exquisite pain and death of the possessor. In the form of its final metaphorization—the sword—the Phallus acquires the name Phalès. The painful, fatal attainment of the absolute is concomitant with the naming and thus the very possession of the fleeting object of desire. Similarly, Marcueil possesses Ellen only subsequent to her "death"-in-love when he renames her "Hélène." Only then did she cease to elude him and only then could he arrest his demonic pursuit of a sexual record. Literality could then metaphorize into absolute eroticism. By (re)naming the Phallus, Messalina assures the eternal presence of the desired object which she finally calls into existence by her verbal act and deifies by means of her self-sacrifice. Whence too the symbolic equivalence of this absolute masculine signifier and Death. Fecundation and murder: opposites are equal.

If the Phallus signifies more than one content, it assumes multiple and contradictory forms as well, one of which is a bird, an appropriate symbol of flight. This beloved but slippery object also appears as the moon—likewise signifying partial and gradual disappearance—and is especially a being of shifting identity. Furthermore, tradition depicts the moon as the Land of the Dead. Significantly, lunar objects have a reflecting capability (mimicking the moon's reflection of sunlight): represented above all by the mirror. Messalina sees the God of Love reflected in a spherical mirror, an object incorporating both the formal and symbolic attributes of the moon, and which signifies the Phallic God. The connotations of the mirror function in conjunction with the problematic of nomination. There is a terrible secret name whose utterance is cause for the Roman death penalty. This forbidden name is disguised by the place-name ROMA. The taboo protects the sacred name of the city's god, a deity who has left his subjects. Messalina, holding the city's medallion up to a golden mirror, reads AMOR. Henceforth she would seek the god AMOR, the god of Love. The mirror moreover signifies the game of absence played by the constantly decamping god and reproduces the very structure of the text: on the level of narrative, the quest for the "always already" absent object of desire; on a semiotic plane, the character of the signifieds which also function as signifiers of new signifieds, the Phallus being only a paradigmatic point in the textual latticework.

Equally important, the sphere—mirror and moon—symbolizes the All. Messalina paradoxically encounters this perfect form as the body of the homosexual mime Mnester, rolled into a ball at the finale of his obscene dance. Thus, the spherical object is clearly sexually charged and, given Mnester's mute performance, embraces the semiological uncertainty of the text exhibited in the game of mirrors.

Finally, Messalina's mother is the bearer of the lethal gift, the giver of the Phallus. Transcultural mother symbols such as the vulture portray the mother figure as Death. Hermetic lore, with which Jarry was acquainted, equates death to a return of the mother. The exit of this deadly mother-phallus (semiologically and psychologically she represents although she cannot possess the phallus), with which the novel concludes, specifies the ultimate absence of the God of Love.

L'Objet aimé, pastoral en un acte [The Beloved Object, Pastoral in One Act]

An example of Jarry's *théâtre mirlitonesque,* this schematic play lends itself to a marionette staging. A *mirliton* is a "reed-pipe" and *vers de mirliton* refers to bad poetry. This categorization by Jarry of some six works (which he linked in a 1906 letter to the *théâtre ubuesque*) might lead one to believe falsely that these works are not serious or that they are carelessly composed.[15] On the contrary, this "mirlitonesque" verse is "an expression intentionally childlike and simplified of the absolute, wisdom of all nations" (423 in "Lecture on Puppets"). For Jarry, the sound of the reed-pipe conjured the profound joy of childhood excursions to the Puppet theater. Indeed, the instrument's power and value make it the perfect offering from Ubu, just ennobled by the King of Poland, to his sovereign (495 in *Ubu Cuckold or the Archeopteryx*). In fact, the *théâtre mirlitonesque* was the mature outgrowth of a type of writing that had already interested Jarry during his adolescence: the style combines lyrical buoyancy and faultless rhythm. The frequent use of nonsense words and the playful manipulation of rhyme to express—in the guise of pastorals and musical comedies—concerns as profound as those of his most esoteric and patently serious works demonstrates a masterful control of language.

Love causes just as much anguish in the *mirlitonesque* play as elsewhere. The quest for the absolute continues by means of the courtship of the "beloved object": as perfect, remote, and unknowable a woman as any fabled princess. In order to possess her, to become one with his object of desire, Monsieur Vieuxbois, the

ludicrous suitor, attempts in vain to reproduce her language. The
Beloved Object sings:

> Sous la charmille
> Que l'aube mouille
> Perle son trille
> Comme il gazouille! (sc. i)

Her lamentable admirer stammers:

> Elle est charmouille . . .
> Non je bafouille:
> Elle est charmante! (sc. i)

His ridiculous scrambling of letters along with his consciousness
of his emotional turmoil present love as a linguistic "tic." Let
there be no mistake, however, regarding the important role of
a "tic" in Jarry's writings. Elsewhere he wrote: "the soul is a
tic."[16] Here is yet another instance of the mechanical gesture
(physical or verbal) acquiring awesome power. The rhetorical
games recall the mechanical deformation of words by the remarkable phonograph in *The Supermale* which hypnotizes Ellen
and the Indian, its bizarre linguistic combinations inducing insanity in Marcueil and announcing Ellen's death. Jarry tellingly
compared the reed-pipe to "a phonograph that brings back to life
the recording of a past" (495): yet another clue to the sober theme
cloaked in buffoonery. For if Monsieur Vieuxbois puts his all into
making the Beloved Object's words his own, his fate is to *be
possessed by* the language of desire, a linguistic "vampire" filling
the void of his own lack of control over language and his inability
to use language-as-power, that is to verbally seduce the desired
Object. For Jarry, farce was serious business.

L'Amour en visites [Love Goes Visiting]: Lucien

This collection of eleven tableaux and dramas features seven
pieces in which Lucien, a brash young bourgeois, visits a series
of females, and one male doctor—needed to treat his resulting

malady. The theme of love reverberates throughout Jarry's opus, each work presenting a variation on love's manifestations. Here, its kaleidoscopic formulations are condensed into a single work. "Linteau" [Lintel] (the preface of *Les Minutes de sable mémorial*) theorizes that words are polyhedral ideas. "Love" as it travels from courtesan to precocious child to fiancée—embodied by an increasingly disillusioned and angry Lucien—leaves no doubt that its initial view as cacography par excellence conceals a coherent and penetrating ontological statement. Whether vulgar or cerebral, immature or sophisticated, sarcastic or serious, absurd or absolute, love represents neither uncontrollable emotional turmoil nor an adamic state of enchantment, but a conscious act of human volition permitting man to triumph over contingency. Each visit love makes reveals a different aspect of it; the lover's perception determines his reality. Thus does love become eroticism ("Visiting the Old Lady"), serious sport ("Visiting the Fiancée"), a battle ("Visiting Manon"), bourgeois pretension and hypocrisy ("Visiting Manette"), or pure childish fantasy ("Visiting the Little Cousin").

The galavanting of the picaresque hero constitutes an unorthodox manual on love become a hyperconnoted signifier. His conventional outings become, on the one hand, unwonted displays of sadism; and on the other, revulsion at institutionalized love: untrustworthy, sterile, and routine. Lucien adds yet another member to the inventory of "deserters" and "assassins": Jarry warns that "the somber expanse of his eyes is filled with disquieting things . . ." (854). This seriousness of purpose is, however, executed with a wink of the eye, for the text is profusely riddled with "black humor." A sinister and self-satisfied smile accompanies Lucien's rapier-sharp yet prancing verbal jibes at social repression of instinctual desires ("Visiting the Grand Lady"), at conventional sexless middle-class family life ("Visiting Manette," the housekeeper), at the soldier-whore syndrome ("Visiting Manon"), at the lascivious seduction of young men by aging women ("Visting the Old Lady"),[17] and at the belittling of young girls' fantasies by pretentious adults ("Visiting the Little Cousin").

Felicity, Lucien's fiancée, does not escape his linguistic and ideological attack. Their confrontation illustrates his tactics. His ironic contempt for bourgeois respectability produces a sarcastic diatribe that is rooted in the Greek etymology of "sarcasm," i.e., *sarkazein:* tearing away flesh or dismemberment. A propitious metaphor equating the maiden to a threatening shark—"the most fearful enemy of humanity" (877)—has a dual function. First, it permits the elaboration of sadistic dental symbolism of which the salient image is the "bite," one of Jarry's pet emblems; second, it creates the desire to harpoon this dangerous female: to sink a fatal barbed spear into her flesh.

Coquettish and insidiously persevering, Felicity, who knows only a spurious existence, would have Lucien join the ranks of genteel citizens. Her beau, however, realizes that he is involved in a struggle for survival. To subdue the false object of desire he must use force, and her subversive sense of propriety mobilizes Lucien to "fight dirty." So as not to risk his own annihilation, he rejects the bourgeois notions of love and marriage and commits his only "reasonable" action since meeting Felicity: he bites her lip and draws blood, informing her that she has been "honorably raped" (875–76). His shocking act catalyzes an increasingly agonistic dialogue which he prudently recognizes as two different languages (878), based on the functional opposition of "biting" (the sign of the nonconformist, the "anarchist" [876]) to "chewing" (the modality of bourgeois virtue). Further exchange of words is literally useless. Only the physical scar will remain: the glyph of Lucien's individuality and freedom.

Laughter, the proof of his invulnerability and escape from the shark-infested waters of feminine wiles, interrupts his venomous discourse. His final speech couples his saliva with his ex-fiancée's blood "to procreate the first bastard" of her clan: "you will give birth to Love," he prophesies, "but I will no longer be there to acknowledge it" (879). Love, born of necessity from aggression and pain, from violated consciousness, and from humiliation, cannot be legitimized. Neither can the so-called Love, cold-blooded and vapid, of the wedding-gown merchants.[18]

La Dragonne [The She-Dragoon]

This is Jarry's last work, cut short by illness and death. It is at once strikingly autobiographical and calculatedly fictionalized. Jarry dreams his life, returning to the "timescape" of his beloved Breton childhood. In April 1903 he had published "La Bataille de Morsang" [The Battle of Morsang], which would become a long and polished chapter of the final work. And during the summer of 1907, just before his death, he was still working on the chapter "Les Crocodiles de Bacchus," giving special attention to the prose poem "Mousse." In the end, he dictated plans for completion of the book to his sister Charlotte, and it seems apt that she should collaborate on this odyssey into the familial past. The novel was not published until 1943, in a particularly faulty version.

Resembling his other works, but to an even greater degree owing to its date and subject, *La Dragonne* spins a web of allusions of Daedalian complexity. The lack of closure which characterizes the novel in a literal way, also characterizes its "unreadability." There is more than one meaning, each intertwined with the other, but never culminating in any logos, any unified, complete meaning for the novel. Like the "inexplicable wall" in "Fear Visiting Love," here too there always remains some mediating sign to obstruct and yet lure the reader. Textual "white outs" disorient the reader who is deliberately left to project himself into both theme and creative plan. This parallels the use of ellipses both with reference to Melusina in *Absolute Love* and as the ongoing "end" of *Faustroll*.

Puzzling and disconcerting, the novel copies its title in a textual strategy used as early as the *Minutes de sable mémorial* (1894). Several readings of the title present themselves immediately, only to be challenged once a reading of the novel reflects back onto them. Thus do title and novel continually reflect one another in a never-ending series of analogies and contradictions. A first interpretation should perhaps address the significance of the dragon. As I have suggested in the analysis of *Absolute Love*, dragons are universal and symbolic figures, characteristically joining disparate elements of aggressive and minatory animals. Rem-

iniscent of the archeopteryx whom Ubu regrets not having
engendered in *Ubu Cuckolded,* the dragon symbolizes instinct and
brutality. A frequent alchemical symbol, it illustrates the stage
of *putrefactio.* As a psychological image, the dragon indicates
disintegration and conquering the dragon implies sublimation.
Jung described the dragon as a mirror of man's unconscious.
Hermetic lore portrays dragons too as forces of darkness, who
represent blind impulse toward gratification and are fought by
sun-heroes. In Christian iconography, the dragon depicts the
demon. In everyday speech *un dragon de vertu* means "a great
prude" (*une femme affectant une vertu farouche*), and thus does this
masculine signifier *un dragon* extend its purview to the female.
The word, however, has an officially feminine form as well: *une
dragonne,* as in the expression *à la dragonne,* meaning in a shrewish
or vixenish manner. Once again the feminine is defined as ve-
nemous and savage. *La dragonne* is also, most obviously, the "she-
dragon."

"To dragoon" has come to mean "to harass" in general, or to
compel to a certain course of acton as if by use of dragoons, as
well as to subject to military persecution. A *dragonnade* refers to
brutal religious persecution, specifically encountered by the
French Huguenots, a Protestant minority in Catholic France
which was combated by Louis XIV's dragoons (musketeers). In
his *Alfred Jarry* (1980), Maurice LaBelle translates the novel's
title *The Persecuted,* forfeiting an important dose of ambiguity,
but emphasizing the unwarranted aggression and suffering. The
dragoon (the persecutor) took his name from his weapon, *la
dragonne,* meaning either the short musket hooked to his belt or
the sword-knot, a leather sling, by which the hilt of a sword was
attached to the wrist. This latter would be ornamented with
tassels tied to the hilt. "Dragoon," then, can be an action, a
combatant, or a weapon (in French as well as in English). The
double-tassled sword, carrying with it all the symbolism of the
dragon and of sexual ambiguity, makes a bizarre and chilling
entrance in Jarry's novel.

A daughter is born to a disappointed Monsieur Martin Paranjeoux-Sabrenas and his wife, Camille, and the military man

names the girl Jeanne in the hope that she will at least live up to her namesake, Jeanne d'Arc. When she reaches a suitable age, her parents find a cavalry dragoon to court her, namely Erbrand Sacqueville. Jeanne, nicknamed Fleur-de-Sabre ("Saber-Flower"), quickly donates her virginity to the troops (the closest she can come to being one of them), and ends up dying impaled, à la Messaline, on Erbrand's sword. Around this drama, Jarry weaves a tale of mythological proportions, beginning with the circumstances of Jeanne's birth. Directly above the newborn's head swung her father's dragoon, bedecked with its double silk braid. The word for "acorn" and "tassle" being the same in French (*gland*) we may assume the ornaments to have some sort of ball-shaped knotted ends. Very graphically, then, the sword cum ornament, attached to the body of the father who is verifying his offspring's sex, constitutes the sign under which Jeanne is born.

Jeanne's identity thus duplicates the neonatal insignia which combines the phallus (sword) and the double (tassle). In her case, the phallic—an economy of power, knowledge, and currency—does not equal the masculine gender.[19] She figures a special brand of the powerful double, personifying an object that is both literally and symbolically potent as well as bifurcated. In much the same way as the dual title *Haldernablou* signified the "double beast coupled with itself" (*la double bête accouplée*) rather than two beasts joined together, the dragoon's tassles are "the double silk braid" (*la double tresse de soie*).[20] Indeed, Jeanne, already identified with the dragoon as phallus and as penis—represented by her hovering father, the (carrier of the) dragoon—joins passionately with the blade possessed by the young dragoon Erbrand. Sacqueville and his weapon are avatars of her own double.

This phallic female's first double (chronologically), Martin Paranjeoux-Sabrenas, in turn the image of his dragoon, relays power to a younger man (mimicking Sengle and Valens) also identified by the dragoon that swings from his belt. It follows that the object of Jeanne's desire—her "beloved object"—is her own double, whence the novel's fundamental structure of mirroring, typical of narcissistic self-love. Jeanne begins life characterized by indeterminate gender, is quickly identified as a female destined to act like a male, and eventually becomes one with the sword *(la dragonne)* which reproduces the one held over her head at birth. Not surprisingly, Jungian psychology interprets the dragon as a mother image: Jeanne continues the Jarryan legacy of the phallic mother.

Erbrand Sacqueville's name, family history reports, comes from Jarry's ancestor, Erbrand de Sacqueville, who accompanied William the Conqueror on his British campaign. The fictional Erbrand, deprived of the aristocratic "de," has a grandfather named Anselme, the name of Alfred Jarry's father. Curiously, the dragoon's father resembles not Anselme Jarry, but Alfred's maternal grandfather. At the *lycée* of Saint-Brieuc, Jarry occasionally encountered his grandfather Charles Jean-Baptiste Quernest, a part-time teacher and former justice of the peace. In the novel, the weekly *lycée* course in legislation is attributed to Erbrand's father. Gustave Sacqueville also shares Charles Quernest's interest in archeology. (It is interesting to note that Jarry had a younger brother, who died an infant, named Gustave Anselme.) Jeanne's relationship with Martin Paranjeoux-Sabrenas parallels this subtle (fictional) elimination of Jarry's father. The name of the father, the patronym, conceals a matrilinear genealogy. Erbrand's name lacks the patrilinear attribution *de* ("of") because his decendency is identified through the matriarchy, the father of the mother. Jeanne's father too is simultaneously masculine and feminine, having affixed by a hyphen his wife's family name (Sabrenas) to his own. Jeanne, or Fleur-de-Sabre, on whom the father pins all his dreams and focuses his desires, assimilates the "mother-become-father" (or maternal father) in the form of a name her military persona acquires.

The father is barred because the phallic (but not castrating) mother (that is, the she-dragoon/she-dragon: the monstrous female serpent) affirms herself. In terms of Freudian syllabic chemistry or of the alphabetical alchemy practiced by Rimbaud, Paranjeoux is, thus, the parent (in French, phonologically, *paran* = "parent") who does not play *(jeoux* = "joue"), unless it is with the X that finishes him off. Moreover, Jeanne's mother's husband is not her biological father, so that she is removed in yet another way from "legitimate" (patrimonial) connection to him. The erasure of the name of the father (Paranjeoux) in the child (Fleur-de-Sabre) corresponds to a complex phenomenon in Jarry's works which links the letter "X" to desire, and, in some respects, resembles the "X" placed over certain words in deconstructive critical maneuvers.[21] In *The She-Dragoon,* the chapter "L'<<X>>" introduces Erbrand Sacqueville.

The father is symbolically absent, marking a (or the) lack at the origin of experience and knowledge. The father/name of the father/phallus exists here only in terms of a trace, effaced in the very act of presenting his/its legibility and legitimacy. In "La" ("the" in its feminine form), a chapter of *Absolute Love,* Emmanuel God's mother kisses him good-bye in a space demarcated by an iron gate: school. The kiss given by the mother who is present marks her absence and his solitude. "Et, la porte ferrée franchie, [. . .], sa solitude s'affirmait du baiser de départ de *sa mère*" (Pléiade, 932; Jarry's emphasis). Because of the "memory of his mother's skirts" and because the little boys wear girls' dresses, he refers to his classmates in the feminine: "*La* Mecqerbac, *la* Zinner, *la* Xavier" (Pléiade, 933; Jarry's emphasis). That year, Emmanuel developed a mania for wooden paperknives which he had his carpenter father fashion for him. Emmanuel, however "perfected them himself, no doubt in the image of the creative saw, voracious and lively, admired on its mahogany roost, by adding hand-saw teeth and the arch of a groove on its back, toward the tip of the word *cutlass* [*coutelas,* a large knife]" (Pléiade, 934; Jarry's emphasis). He brandishes the finished product, calling it a "torture stick" (reminiscent of the *bâton-à-physique*), while surreptitiously spying on his friend Xavier for the greater part of an evening. The entire experience of that school year became definitively condensed into this boy, whose features were forgotten, replaced by the first letter of his name, by the "trace of the X that whitens, at the portals of burials, under the human heads of wall-hangings: *La* Mecqerbac, *la* Zinner, *la* . . . La Mort" (Pléiade, 934). So that "Death" *(Mort)* displaces "X" and both are symbolized by the creative, if dangerous, saw.

La Dragonne is part of the same system in which sexual indeterminacy and deconstruction of gender (and traditional phallogocentrism) are linked to a killing that is accomplished by means of effacement, erasure, or "whitening" but is also coextensive with the saw-toothed knife (in *Absolute Love*) or the dragoon. In both cases, the name of the male (Xavier; Paranjeoux) is erased; but strangely, the unusual feminine component remains: "La"; "Sabre." The trace is associated with death, as when "Xavier" is first reduced to "X," the symbol of erasure, to be ultimately replaced by "Death" following the feminine article "la" (in the series "La Mecqerbac, la Zinner, la . . . La Mort"). Death stands on equal terms with the feminine, this last no longer emphasized by italics. Death, though, as iconized by Emmanuel's knife (and the dragoon) is "creative," "voracious," and "lively." So too the play of presence and absence of the deconstructive "X."

In "L'<<X>>," fourth chapter of Part I of *The She-Dragoon,* Erbrand Sacqueville makes his appearance following the initiatory words: "then the adventure commenced" (46). This pronouncement is preceded by "distant and unreal" noises, those of a tugboat scraping its anchor under the water of the river along which stroll Jeanne and her parents. Such sounds signal, here as elsewhere in Jarry's writings, the presence of the double (the presence of what can only be absence, non-being). Erbrand, mounted and in uniform, described as having eyes that see far (87)—identifying him as belonging to the clan of Sengle and Marcueil—makes his entrance then, under the sign of the "X." Here as in *Absolute Love,* the "X" is associated with the first year of school ("L'X" is the nickname of the Polytechnique), described in terms of captivity and revolt (be it anarchy or desertion): presence and absence. Thus, Erbrand's initiation into a corpus of knowledge, of signification, and Jeanne's "initiation" to Erbrand both fall under the "X." One aspect of revolt against school is playfully and ironically described as adherence to "Ibsenism." Ibsen, the avant-garde dramatist, appealed to Jarry; *Faustroll* translates the importance of Jarry's performance in his *Peer Gynt.* The irony is sustained when Erbrand is said to be the antithesis of a man of letters, even being contemptuous of such people. The statement is ironic for Erbrand is in every way a man of *the* letter: "X," the sign of absence, the sign of the absent father, the sign of the affirmative phallic mother, the sign of desire.

The problematical status of this letter and its function in the text relate to the status of the double and self-love. Doubling structures the relationship between Jeanne and Erbrand. Double by virtue of her birth sign, Jeanne accepts the fate of being "blessed" with "that precious and double quality" of being a bastard child of a lord and a harlot (37). Her non-father, Paranjeoux-Sabrenas, knows well the feeling of psychic schism. "For him, the officer was a being apart, exterior to himself, the civilian Paranjeoux. He would 'see him coming,'—better yet, he would go to look for him, he would choose him" (34). In imitation of his future father-in-law, Erbrand (on the battlefield) fabricates a dragoon from pink silk, like the ornament positioned over Jeanne's head and like the driver's mask worn by Ellen Elson when she arrived at Marcueil's in full regalia as his female counterpart. Finishing his ornament just in the nick of time, Erbrand hears a lieutenant order an attack; when their ammunition runs out, the "biting of bayonetes" follows (91).

Dental sadism and devouring—the erotics of doubling—had already opened the novel. Snow-capped peaks surrounding the embattled village of Morsang resemble the Freudian toothed vagina of the phallic mother and set the scene (as they do in "The Old Man of the Mountain," where the jagged range surrounds Paradise) for seduction, combat, and death-in-love with one's double. In the midst of a ceasefire, a small altar is set up, compared to an "armoire with two opened doors" (19–20). The décor, then, places this sacred diptych—replete with the symbolism of the opened book/hand imagery of *The Other Alceste*—in the center of an area that seems "devoured by an always gaping jaw" (19), that of the mountains. Doubling, the sacred, dental sadism, mirror-images, and death converge in the scene of a duel between Erbrand and another soldier just before the arrival of a priest (107–8). Furthermore, the visual component of the duel figures the "X" of two crossed swords. The sword (here called *le sabre*) is a "*bâton* that cuts only under certain conditions," thus establishing parity among the dragoon, Fleur-de-Sabre, and the *bâton-à-physique*. Erbrand assimilates blows to his stomach by the *bâton* that "bounces in decreasing jumps" (like the uprooted Phallus in *Caesar-Antichrist*, who is admonished not to jump up and down), to unpleasant caresses. The *bâton-à-physique*, as portrayed in *Caesar-Antichrist*, also depicts the "X" when rotating on its axis, unifying the plus and minus signs into the hermaphrodite or the Androgyn, the bisexual being also embodied by the phallic mother. The "certain conditions" under which the phallus "cuts" are indeed special, for they signal the presence of the double.

Following the duel in which he commits ritualized murder, Erbrand perceives the black silhouette of a man which seems to him like a mastodon, an extinct elephantlike animal whose distinguishing feature is molar teeth. Thus, the dental, the giant shadow-image, and extinction combine in a dangerous game of presence and absence. The large man clothed in black is a priest whose vocation is described as being other than what he is (112). Erbrand sympathizes with the priest's feeling of alterity, having himself experienced the same phenomenon (like Paranjeoux-Sabrenas, who considers his military side a being apart). The speech Erbrand makes to the priest sounds curiously similar to the oft-cited letter Jarry wrote to Rachilde: "We have catalogued into three classes the vagaries of dead peoples' fantasies. We discipline their dreams, which are the only Other World. The decomposition of their brains organizes Eternity" (114). Death and decomposition, then, are further emphasized as productive and constitutive of a parallel existence.

Rather than confess directly to the priest, Erbrand places his "confession" (115; quotation marks are Jarry's), also referred to as his "manuscript," in an empty bottle and seals the bottle with great care. Like the parchment entrusted to the waves in "Amber," this manuscript is tossed into a river in a "bottle, carrier of words, resembling a large ovary of waterlilies or the upper jaw of a crocodile" (118). Ovoid shapes were important in "Amber" as well, symbolizing the female and fertility. The jaw imagery, all too obvious, also reproduces the description of Ubu (Pléiade, 467). If the bottle is equivalent to the ubuesque jaw, its con-

tents—the confessional written word—must equal Ubu's nourishment: *phynance/merdre/cervelle.* This is not the sole entry of Ubu
and his world into this "autofictive" novel. The bottle traverses
the concentric circles created in the river by the sinking priest,
killed by Erbrand Sacqueville. The priest's never completed final
utterance, "at the beginning, God's Spirit floated . . ." (118),
ironically predicts that "the bottle, thrown in after him, floated"
(118). It floated "toward mankind." Erbrand's manuscript and
God's spirit are identical; his sacred "words" *(paroles)* are carried
farther and farther across an ever-widening series of circles in the
water: their center, a bubble, must be the escaping soul of the
priest, according to the symbolism of *The Other Alceste.* Their
circumference grew so large that "it was no longer *nowhere (nulle
part)*" (118; my emphasis). The confessional manuscript (that is,
this novel itself) goes beyond "nowhere," *beyond* never-never land:
the French double-negative *ne fût plus nulle part* underscores the
extremity of this position. *The She-Dragoon* goes beyond Pataphysics, beyond the supplementary universe, taking a spasmic
leap into the brain's decomposition in death.

Elements of the *Ubu* texts exist here to deconstruct the system
they represent, a system which also operates in this novel. These
texts incorporate elements of the universe they would "dynamite"
and surpass (and not simply oppose or replace)—such as the
opinions voiced by the Financiers and the Magistrates regarding
Ubu's rampage, or the advice of his Conscience. *The She-Dragoon*
incorporates a rejection of the universe constituted by the supplementary universe only to deconstruct this negation in turn,
to place it, so to speak, under the "X." By going beyond the
double negative Jarry produces an affirmative discourse. The
ubuesque jaw does not devour the autobiographical fiction.

Having sent forth his scriptures, Erbrand searches the battlefield for his fiancée, whom he compares to a veinstone or matrix
(une gangue)—the material in which a gem is embedded; also the
womb—in a garbage heap. His search (poking his sword among
the bodies), the uncanny encounter with the priest, the drowning,
the bottle adrift, all these events occur at night. With dawn's
arrival, Erbrand sees less clearly than before, for he operates in

the same temporal dimension as Sengle, the deserter. Specifically, "the moon was erased" (119). The effect on Erbrand is unexpected: he disrobes. Paradoxically, his nudity acts like a disguise, and Jeanne, not recognizing him, shoots him. When he turns and sees her, he perceives "the indigo and madder-colored disguise *(le travesti)* of Fleur-de-Sabre" (120). The doubles come face to face in much the same way as do Marcueil and Ellen in the *Supermale.* They share a private code that reverses standard values: "for her nudity was being in uniform. In it she found something other than the fiancé she had known clothed, and the same thing, if not better, that she looked for in all men" (121). Despite her search for this masculine "thing," Jeanne protects herself with a revolver against rape. A surprised Erbrand reminds her of her exploits with the soldiers. This reference to her alter ego causes her to speak in codewords similar to the "Indian celebrated by Theophrastes," uttered to mark Ellen's intimacy with Marcueil. In an effort to exculpate herself, she points out, "And above all, you knew very well that my name is Jeanne, like the *other* one" (121; Jarry's emphasis), to which Sacqueville responds, "Je-hanne," modifying her name the same way Marcueil altered Ellen's to "Hélène" (in both cases adding the letter "h" an allusion, perhaps, to Jarry's poem "L'homme à la hache," or the statement that the "juxtaposition of the two signs [minus and plus] yields the letter H, which is Chronos, the father of Time or Life" [Pléiade, 730]). It is all the more ironic that Erbrand rejected the belles-lettres, when once again he proves himself the consummate manipulator of letters, like Jarry, who added the infamous "r" to Ubu's expletive.

The letter is the sign of the Other: just before Caesar-Antichrist announces his departure and the coming of the terrestrial regime (that is, Ubu's), the Templar announces, "I am going to change my being, because the sign alone exists *(he breaks the staff of his cross)* provisionally . . . rest is change" (Pléiade, 292). The Other is called into being, by provisionally negating the letter "X" (of the cross) and then affirming the identity of opposites, thereby negating the double negative. The Other, in this case King Ubu, accedes to being by virtue of yet another game of letters in which three heraldic escutcheons arrange themselves to spell "you" in response to Ubu's question, "Who will be king?"

The meeting between a naked Erbrand and a blue and red uniformed Jehanne, then, ends with the lethal penetration of the girl by the soldier's dragoon, "the sword that had penetrated her—in another way" (127). Now a third offering is made to the river: Jeanne floats. A strange silhouette is formed by her breasts and a flower caught in the lace on her cleavage, a silhouette tracing a "phallic trinity" (128). The "weighty emblem," arched like a "vanquished saber," seems to sink the body. In death she literally becomes her name, Saber-Flower, which signifies, provisionally, the sacred phallus; and it was her undoing. The matrix and the sacred phallus, Jeanne and Jehanne, the split emblem of the phallic mother, is, so to speak, violated to death (like the girl on the grounds of the Supermale's mansion) by her double, *la dragonne.* Only by being deflowered by the saber (which inherits her virginity [p. 128]) can she be Saber-Flower. This mode of writing deconstructs from within the system of metaphysics which rejects (represses, in psychoanalytic terms) any threat to the presence of the logos. In "The Battle of Morsang," reference to meaning and to an order of signification (the logocentric system) is subverted by a type of "double writing," or writing simultaneously in two different codes. The codes are neither parallel nor consecutive, but rather intertwined like the wool in a skein, as the doubles slip in and out of roles and as the mirror-images metamorphose.

Furthermore, in death, Jeanne resembles the "wreckage where kings, on the Seine, used to sign laws on a writing-board" (128). She herself is the fact of the deconstructive inscription; she *is* the boundless fluidity of the written sign, of the signature on the water, of the confessional manuscript carried by the water, of the feminine waters inscribed by the identity of opposites. The "X," no longer broken, as by the Templar (in *Caesar-Antichrist*), blossoms on the wreckage of the phallogocentric sign: "L'épave, avec cette hampe fleurie plantée" replaces "il brise la hampe de sa croix." The stalk of man is no longer castrated (no longer "uprooted"); implanted in woman, it takes root and flowers.

This image relays to that of Antaeus's omnipotent mother: part III, the last section of the *She-Dragon,* opens with the figure of a son entirely dependent upon his mother for strength and vitality. Entitled "Antaeus," it fuses Erbrand's return to Brittany, the land of his childhood, and the Greek myth of Antaeus, a giant wrestler invincible while touching the earth, his mother, but strangled by Hercules while the latter held him off the ground. Antaeus is invoked when Erbrand makes contact with the earth again, walking off the moving train carrying him back in space—and time—to Brittany.

Antaeus links the Greek myth of the all-powerful mother to the bisexual hermaphrodite who engenders everything and to a haunting past which posits one universal language:

> Antée! paronymes have a mysterious and clear meaning for whoever knows how to interpret them, and plays on words are not play. Antaeus is the spouse of Antea. His past—or rather he is the past himself, formidable hermaphrodite, generator of all things. Yesteryear [*antan*], to haunt [*hanter*], his uncle and first teacher the Abby Saint-Pligeaux, had taught him that for whoever knows how to read, there is only one tongue in the world and that for that person, there was never a Babel. (130)

Awaiting him at the train station, Erbrand's maternal grandmother personifies this tripartite organization. The wife of General Ermelinaye is referred to as *la générale,* echoing the sexual confusion and duality implied in the expression *la dragonne* and by the hermaphrodite mentioned in connection with Antaeus. In her antiquated carriage, Erbrand's grandmother is a sign of the past, metonymic of absence, in the same way that *la dragonne* recalls *la dragonnade* (an historical episode of persecution) and that the mythological "Anteus" leads to "Antan," "hanter," and the avuncular teacher. Linguistically, she represents Breton, the langauge of Britanny, spoken as a "means of remaining impenetrable" (132). So too the passwords exchanged between the dragoon and Jehanne and the unknowable pre-Babel world. Grandmother and grandson do not cross paths at the station. Erbrand heads for home, and immediately seeks out his maternal grandfather, the sexually ambivalent figure of kinship. This effort to relive Erbrand's and Jarry's childhood corresponds to a return to the figure of the masculine in the maternal—implying the absent father—and to the infantile self-image captured forever, captured before separation from the mother, and in a visual, preverbal stage: his maternal grandfather was one of the first to like photography (131). Also enamored of images, Grandfather Charles Quernest wrote a letter to his beloved Charlotte upon the birth of her brother Alfred. Adorned with colorful decals of flowers, birds, butterflies, and puppets, which served not only as decoration but as replacements for words, the letter—like Anselme Sacqueville's snapshots—enciphers that return (to the narcissistic stage of the image and the mother) and that absence (of the stage of language and the father).

Chapter Six
Progeny and Premonition

Alfred Jarry's influence on succeeding generations of writers is both explicit, in the sense of direct recognition by his literary heirs, and implicit, in the sense of creating a climate propitious for experiments in textual production and for changes in conceptual foundations. Implicit, too, in the sense of demonstrating an artistic intuition of a *Zeitgeist*, an instinctive anticipatory sensitivity to modern consciousness.

Much critical attention has been devoted to Jarry's role in avant-garde theater, and specifically to his fathering of the Theater of the Absurd. It is commonplace to name him a forerunner of Surrealism. No recognition, however, has been granted his remarkable prescience in the writing of prose fiction. For Jarry, by the turn of the century, had already developed aspects of narrative today considered ultramodern and, indeed, necessary for a novel to be relevant to our age.

From Jarry to the Theater of the Absurd

Ubu's legacy traces its iconoclastic path through Dadaism, Futurism, Surrealism, and Artaud's Theater of Cruelty, to the Theater of the Absurd. Generally speaking, this theater, is sensorial, irrational, provocative, and given to "black humor." The Dadaists perceived a kindred spirit in Jarry owing to his treatment of language, his desire to shock, and his allegories of the precarious superficiality of grotesque social conditioning. They continued his demystification of morality, patriotism, religion, and logical thought. The Futurists, led by Marinetti, sympathized with Jarry's passion for machines and contemporary scientific discoveries. For the Surrealists, Jarry was an unknowing champion of the unconscious, and Ubu "the magisterial incarnation of the Nietzchean-Freudian id which designates the combination of unknown, unconscious, repressed forces."[1]

Antonin Artaud founded (in 1927) the "Théâtre Alfred Jarry" in honor of a man whose aesthetic program explored the agony and dark laughter elicited by the encounter with one's doubles. Artaud's celebrated theoretical text, *The Theater and Its Double* (1938) calls for a theater of myth, magic, and supraverbal communication capable of rendering tangible man's inner demons. It demands a therapeutic enactment which denies the spectator all reassurance.

Finally, the Theater of the Absurd, exemplified by Eugene Ionesco, Samuel Beckett, Arthur Adamov, and Roland Dubillard, developed the brand of tragicomedy characteristic of Jarry's plays: man, forced to confront his schizoid world, his fears and alienation, his uncertain identity, and his revolting corporeality, finds release in uneasy laughter. Such a discharge of tension can derive from various techniques, for example endless waiting or endless repetition, an inexplicable disproportion between man and his surroundings, loss of memory, or physical ineptitude. The self-conscious decor is nonmimetic, synecdochical, suggestive: this theater shows itself as theater, as artifice.

Writers such as Guillaume Apollinaire, Raymond Roussel, Tristan Tzara, Georges Ribemont-Dessaignes, Jacques Vaché, and Arthur Cravan appreciated the destructive potentialities incarnated by Ubu, his disquieting though comical power of annihilation. Like Jarry, these Dadaists dispensed with a subtle attack on naturalistic theater, typical of Symbolist dramaturgy, in favor of a radical assault. By means of paradox and contradiction they too pataphysically denied the existence of opposites. In *Les Mammelles de Tiresias* [The Breasts of Tiresias] (written 1903, performed 1917), for example, Apollinaire created an extraordinary couple, reminiscent of Marcueil and Ellen: a woman (transformed into a man) and her husband produce 40,050 children in one day. The husband calls himself a "woman-gentleman" and his wife a "man-lady."[2] Creation immediately follows imagination: to make a child-journalist the Husband mixes ink (for blood), a giant pen (for a spinal column), a jar of glue (he needs brains in order not to think), and scissors (for a tongue). Many images—the locomotive, sneezes, balloons flying away—were favorites of Jarry's. Apollinaire joyfully transposes Jarry's *"merdecin"* (a combination of *merde* = "shit" and *médecin* = "physician") into *"mère des seins"* ("mother of the breasts"). Semiotic experimentation, fundamental to Jarry's dramaturgy, subverts the status of the referent, that is, extralinguistic reality: such neologisms ably serve this purpose. Neological signifiers undermine reference and sense.

In the same spirit but with a different tone, in *L'Etoile au front* [Star on the Forehead, 1924], Roussel, à la Jarry, has Indian twins recount the story of a peace-maker, "son of a Russian and a Hindu, as his eyes cried out, one, the most septentrional blue, contrasted with the other, whose deep black breathed the tropics."[3] Justice issues from this male, at once dual and reconciliatory, whose eyes identify his being. Not surprisingly, the play's title refers to the sublime marking of a great creator.

Cocteau, another vehement opponent of realist theater, wished to substitute a "poetry of theater" for "poetry in the theater."[4] In *Parade* (1917), *Le Boeuf sur le toit* [The Ox on the Roof, 1920] and *Les Mariés de la Tour Eiffel* [Eiffel Tower Wedding Party, 1921], familiar objects are defamiliarized, clichés rejuvenated, and stereotypical ideas and actions reorganized into a mental construct recognized by Cocteau as "willful absurdity."[5] The phonograph progressively fetishized by Jarry as the commanding disembodied (or beheaded) voice becomes a main character (played by human actors) under Cocteau's pen. Cocteau shows a penchant as well for the separation of head from body to symbolize the advent of the irrational and anti-intellectual: in *The Ox on the Roof* a barman illegally selling alcohol (insisting on the right of individual intoxication) to a policeman pours gin directly into his customer's body, having beheaded him by lowering a ceiling fan. A desire to portray grotesque dehumanization explains the phenomena of humans rendered inanimate and horrifying, coupled with animation of the décor. The mask, so important to Jarry's dramaturgy, becomes, in *The Ox on the Roof,* enormous cardboard heads. This valorization weds the commonplace to the quintessential, illustrating what Jarry called "condensed complexity." Cocteau's pet metaphors, the mirage and the circus, mirror the Jarryesque hallucination, at once immobile and dynamic, enticing and ephemeral, omnipresent and illusory.

During the "Great Dada Season" of 1921, Tzara's *Le Coeur à gaz* [The Gas Heart] dramatized the functioning human body, a body so mechanized and objectified that the characters were but its parts, played by Tzara and his cohorts. The automatism of a gas heart symbolizes disdained social and linguistic conventions. "Justice" is dismissed as a "nervous tic."[6] Tzara's disarticulation of language mimics Ubu's: compare Tzara's "le physicien pourra dire que c'est la valise qui a volé le voleur. La valse marchait toujours—c'est toujours qui ne marchait plus—il valsait" to Ubu's "ainsi que le coquelicot et le pissenlit à la fleur de leur âge sont fauchés par l'impitoyable faucheur qui fauche impitoyablement leur pitoyable binette,—ainsi le petit Rensky a fait le coquelicot."[7] Linguistic delirium translates the sense of uncontrollable irrationality characterizing, in the opinion of these vanguard writers, the period featuring World War I. Logical communication seemed impossible. Indeed, the finale of Tzara's seventh Dada manifesto repeats the word "scream" (*hurle*) two hundred times.[8] In the *Manifesto of Monsieur aa the antiphilosopher,* he insists that every action be a "cerebral shooting of the revolver."[9] "Aa" is, in *Faustroll,* the usual utterance of the servant Bosse-de-Nage: the pronunciation of "Ha Ha!" in French. Specifically, when pronounced quickly, "it is the idea of unity. Slowly, of duality, of the echo, of distance, of symmetry, of size and duration, of the two principles of good and evil."[10] Is it not then appropriate that Tzara's antiphilosopher share with Jarry's baboon the sign which neutralizes oppositions—thus doing violence to logical thought—and thus signifies the very ballistic capability of the mind for which Tzara campaigned? André Breton knowingly nicknamed Jarry "celui qui révolver."

A similar furious and poetic semiological "blast" characterizes *L'Empereur de Chine* [The Emperor of China], a masterpiece of Dada theater, written in 1916 by Georges Ribemont-Dessaignes.

A composite of fragments—copying both the physical fragmentation resulting from warfare and the shattered syntax of man's unsuccessful efforts to communicate rationally—enacts legitimized incest, rape, assassination, and generalized cruelty. In this play, the Sons of Heaven can no longer communicate with God since their intermediary, the lawful Emperor, was destroyed. The new Emperor, after an Ubuesque rampage, beheads himself and subsequently functions in an absurdly automatic way. There is of course no salvation. Instead, there is on the one hand a philosophy expounded by two clowns, named Equinox and Irony, who simultaneously affirm the "yes" and the "no," the equality and superimposition of opposites; on the other hand, a typewriter (this writing machine harks back to Jarry's cosmogonic painting machine in *Faustroll*) creates a new cacography replacing the Gospel with the new Dada religion: "joy of the inventor" and "perpetual motion"[11] (the same Jarry dreamed of producing with Perpetual-Motion-Food in the *Supermale?*).

Following in Jarry's footsteps, on the one hand, Ribemont-Dessaignes depicts the void materially. No longer metaphysical (as in traditional, transcendent theater), nothingness is "incarnated" on stage and is communicated visually, not conceptually, because scenic images rather than philosophy nourish this type of dramaturgy. On the other hand, this macabre farce thematizes the supremacy of individual freedom and the power of language to create a new order. In *Le Bourreau de Péru* [The Hangman of Peru, 1928], Ribemont-Dessaignes illustrates this power by enlarging the scope of the typewriter metaphor: here, it alone knows everything.[12] The machine replaces the human brain so that an executioner may punish "virtual" crimes. The very definition of Pataphysics stresses the "virtual" and, of course, the machine and the brain were favorite puppets in Jarry's hands.

Dada, a cultural movement born in a Zurich cabaret during World War I, packed for Paris at the war's end. Some participants of the Zurich activities, however, moved to Berlin and Munich to espouse the maiden school of German Expressionism. With Yvan Goll's Dada-Expressionist *Malthusalem ou l'éternal bourgeois* [Malthusalem or the Eternal Bourgeois] (written in 1919) the

Ubu character appears domesticated but in fact has only switched roles with his double. Here, Malthusalem's double, animated in celluloid dreams projected on stage, represents base instinct. The anguish and confusion of an unstable self are incongruously portrayed by grotesque caricatural masks.

For historical reasons, the violence and aggression fundamental to Dadaism and the political concerns of most Expressionist plays seem far more anguished—despite frequent music-hall or clowning techniques—than the more philosophical anarchy typical of Jarry's writings. Like their predecessor, though, the Dadaists and the Dada-Expressionists counterbalanced their serious message with outrageous, delirious humor.

The Surrealists tempered Dada's radical and systematic nihilism as well as its gratuitous spontaneity. With Breton the Dada current became intellectualized. Unconscious depths were sounded for liberating, curative potentialities. Ensuing experiments with automatic writing combined badly, however, with the exigencies of dramatic structure. Although the Surrealists paid homage to Jarry, it was primarily those who left the movement or were peripheral to it who were more fertile in the domain of theater.

In 1924 René Daumal and Roger Gilbert-Lecomte wrote a series of Jarryesque short plays glorifying nonsense. They were published collectively as *Petit Théâtre* [Little Theater] by the College of Pataphysics. Gilbert-Lecomte followed Jarry's program for pushing life to its limits: he systematically committed "suicide" never actually dying from his experiments but glimpsing other realms in the process. A similar afficionado of the pataphysical, Julien Torma (if he really existed), left his Alpine hotel one fine day and disappeared forever. After Jarry, the publications of the College of Pataphysics devote most ink to Torma. His play *Le Bétrou* features acts numbered from minus three to zero. It destroys the distinction between life and death while at the same time accusing language of impotence. The inadequacies of language also concerned Vitrac, one of the few truly successful dramatists to emerge from the Surrealist group. His *Les Mystères de l'amour* [Mysteries of Love] chaotically mixes the real with the dream, dispensing with chronology. A self-commentary on the need to invent a new dramatic tongue, this play is clearly an immediate precursor of the Theater of the Absurd. Vitrac's *Victor, ou les enfants au pouvoir* [Victor, or the Children Wield Power] anticipates Ionesco's nightmarish farces.

For Artaud, theater would make manifest the underlying terror of an inauthentic, dispossessed, fragmented existence. Innocent, primary, preverbal or infantile mental processes would clear the path for ultimate psychic wholeness. Chaos, necessarily, would be incorporated into the performance. Like Jarry, Artaud loathed the "putrefaction of Reason. Logical Europe endlessly crushes the spirit between the hammers of two limits."[13] He too wished to become one with his double; his alchemical quest toward unity also required destruction en route—systematic, provocative, and poetic.

André Green has astutely recognized that this type of theater is not a theater of anxiety due simply to historical events in the modern world. He points out that history has known other anxiety-ridden periods. He characterizes this brand of theater as "post-Freudian," in the sense of depicting "processes whose formal characteristics Freud has stated." Post-Freud theater, of which Jarry was an intuitive precursor, is one of "desire, of the primary process which tends toward discharge (hence, the role of spontaneity, of crisis), which is ignorant of time and space (theatre of ubiquity and non-temporality), which abandons the requirements of logic (theatre of contradiction) and, lastly, a theatre of condensation and displacement (theatre of symbolization)."[14]   •

The journey from Jarry to the Theater of the Absurd includes changes in notions of language, character, staging (directing, acting, décor, audience), and vision of the world. The theater would no longer serve as a pleasing divertissement or elevating experience. The pervasive humor of the avant-garde was not meant to mitigate a malign view of life (symbolized by Ubu). As Martin Esslin has written, the definition of Pataphysics is essentially "the definition of a subjectivist and expressionist approach that exactly anticipates the tendency of the Theater of the Absurd to express psychological states by objectifying them on stage."[15]

Thus, Jarry's philosophical, aesthetic, and technical innovations came to fruition during the half-century following his death in 1907. Today we are accustomed to irreverent and malleable language, to verbal delirium, to questioning the viability and the vitality of language, to spectator participation, to tragicomedy, to psychodrama, to "happenings." It no longer seems radical to loose unrecognizable characters who dialogue with their doubles in atemporal and unlocalizable settings; to stage verbal and scenic collages; to enact alienation, derangement, or incoherent rage; to favor poetic images rather than discursive forms. Jarry left a rich heritage of concretely visualized psychic fury and dispossession. He inaugurated a theater painfully and painstakingly self-conscious in its desire to destroy scenic illusion in order to assert its immanence—its very theatricality—and to deny the spectator his "otherness" by simultaneously forcing him to enter the play's workings and to abandon the search for the play's "true" meaning. He launched the horror and tense hilarity of a clown who incarnates a schizoid, hypocritical, anthropophagic society. Dramatists from Apollinaire, Julien Torma, and Boris Vian to Michel de Ghelderode, Arthur Adamov, and Romain Weingarten, to name but a few, have inherited Jarry's aesthetic of surprise and violent rupture, of elliptical incongruity and profanity. The aspects of puppetry utilized in Jarry's dramaturgy continued to influence his successors. His sinister and vengeful laughter reverberates throughout the twentieth century's avant-garde plays; it represents the forces of freedom. Perhaps the most significant legacy Jarry left in the area of theatricality concerns language: its "pathological" forms, its "literality" (or the literal value of figurative speech), and its essential and very disconcerting ambiguity.

From Jarry to the "Modern" Novel

Martin Esslin concluded as well that Jarry "must be regarded as one of the originators of the concepts on which a good deal of contemporary art, and not only in literature and the theater, is based."[16] What, in fact, are Jarry's credits as a forerunner of writers of modern or contemporary literature, and especially fiction? "Modern" is applied today, logically, to what has been influenced by twentieth-century developments such as Einstein's theory of relativity, Freud's theories on dreams and the unconscious, the concepts of the closed field in mathematics, montage in the cinema, and a variety of cameras (such as the "time-lapse") and lenses (such as the "zoom") in photography.[17] For structuralist Jonathan Culler, the touchstones of "modernism"—system, relation, and relativity—apply to areas as seemingly diverse as linguistics, painting, physics, sociology, psychoanalysis, and literature.[18] Rather than seeking to represent the familiar or, at least, the recognizable, modern literature shows more concern for the relations among textual elements, for a "system" of "underlying functions," and for the effects of combinatory processes such as juxtaposition. The interrelation between desire and violence, for example, would interest the modernist—as it did Jarry—and not a portrayal of an historically believable courtship or job hunt.

In 1968, in *The Novel of the Future,* Anaïs Nin remarked, "In films we accepted the abrupt transitions, jump cutting, fadeouts, flashbacks, fluid dream sequences, superimposition of images."[19] She counseled, "The novelist of the future, like the modern physicist, knows that a new psychological reality can be explored only under new conditions of atmospheric pressure, temperature, and speed, as well as in terms of new time and space dimensions for which the old forms and conventions of the novel are completely inadequate."[20] New forms manipulate obscurity, nihilism, primitivism, dislocation of conventional syntax, and ambiguity.[21] While Jarry did not, of course, construct his novels exclusively in a "modern" way, he *did* illustrate many modernist theories and techniques with pertinent examples and use narrative to describe or to comment on such potential developments.

Nonlinearity, discontinuity, lability, and fragmentation organize novels which represent the epistemological profile of modern fiction.[22] Realism is no longer mimesis of so-called "reality," but rather an exploration of models of information or forms of intelligibility where the real is produced.[23] "Truth" can be only relative, partial, and ambiguous. Fugacity and indeterminacy, symptomatic of modern uneasiness, thus contribute to the formal as well as thematic elements of a new realism.

Jarry's novels are actually among the first to reject chronological sequence, environmental and psychological verisimilitude, motivation for characters and action, characters recognizable in terms of history or geography—in short, all aspects of realism and logic typical of his century's novels. Of chief importance, however, is his spatialization of time. In modern physics time becomes a function of space understood as dynamic. This means that space exists relative to a mobile point of view, and is no longer conceived in a flat or linear perspective. Jarry's comments on the shape of a watchface—an object that literally represents time in terms of spatial relations—demonstrate his grasp of this phenomenon: "Why does everyone claim that the shape of a watch is round, which is manifestly false, since in profile one perceives a narrow rectangular form, elliptical from a three-quarter view, and why the devil has its shape been noticed only when we look at the time?"[24] Here, he foreshadows modern novelists who deny the authenticity of an absolute vantage point, and he uses the same irony, plural and uncertain points of view, and other indications of a fragmented subject which sabotage the modern narrator's authority. *The Supermale,* for example, has a double ending separated by a dotted line: Marcueil's is tragic, Ellen's melodramatic. Faustroll "ends" with an ellipsis, while *Days and Nights* concludes deceptively with the novel quoting itself.

Equally important in subverting linearity, and therefore traditional narration, is the use of juxtaposition. Both post-Freudian exploration of dreams and post-Eisensteinian montage technique of filmmaking challenged writers of fiction. This technique is an organizational mode of motion pictures which arranges sequences of shots from various perspectives. The great Russian filmmaker and theorist Sergei Eisenstein envisioned montage as the juxtaposition of colliding perspectives in which the final composition results from combining conflicting points of view. Eisenstein believed film and literature to be intimately related: shots and words combine similarly to produce a concept, dynamically surpassing both elements of the original dialectic.[25] By eliminating logical transitions, connections of cause and effect, and one-directional action moving from beginning to middle to end, novelists create prose collages. Like dreams and film, novels could thus communicate temporal and spatial simultaneity. One may be "here" and "elsewhere" at the same time or experience more than one "time" without changing location. Various identities might also exist simultaneously. Characters in modern novels are, in fact, often two-sided. Resemblance and contiguity, not sequentiality or causality, characterize modern thought and sensibility, and in fiction juxtaposition translates multiple and complementary or conflicting points of reference.

Jarry's characters represent a simultaneous projection of his own multiple, dynamic personality. Even in his schoolboy plays, he placed special emphasis on "polyhedra": multifaceted solids which can never be totally perceived from any one viewing point. One must imagine the simultaneity of all perspectives to comprehend or apprehend the whole. The polyhedra symbolize not only the sum of the author's "personae" embodied by his fictional characters and multifaceted reality itself, but also—representing solidified concepts in *Ubu Cuckolded*—herald the modern penchant for objectification of the subjective. Modern fiction is consequently often abstract and, paradoxically, intimate. Sengle, Faustroll, Emmanuel God, and Marcueil, all exemplify this unorthodox concept of characterization, and all participate in or articulate such phenomena. As Freud wrote in 1908, the modern novelist tends to shatter his self by auto-observation. These "partial" selves are personified by diverse heroes who represent conflicting currents in an individual's psychic life.

Marcueil, for example, is not only an athletic record breaker, but is also a champion at changing identities. Sengle's ruse is to habitually conjure his past in the form of his "brother." In the same way as an objectified memory taking the form of another character, a locale can metaphorize a mental state. Faustroll, as he travels "forward" through memory, visits islands having no counterparts in geographic reality. The islands constitute moments of his past occurring "realistically" in time and not space. Such exterior spatialization occupies Emmanuel God, who, anticipating modern narrators, projects characters in his own fictional universe who give form to his desires.[26]

Jean-Paul Sartre, in a 1947 discussion of François Mauriac's novels, announced the demise of the "privileged observer" in the novel and compared the novelistic world to Einstein's.[27] This means that the "true" modern novel houses apparently autonomous characters whose inner lives unfold only through what they say or do, rather than via an omniscient narrator. Ultimately, according to this line of thought, there would be ontological equality between the author and his autonomous character: Jarry had already created Ubu, who, in a dazzling sleight of hand, is cited—in *Faustroll*—as the author of *Caesar-Antichrist*. Not to be outdone, Emmanuel God creates Miriam, his object of desire, and in the process reveals his sexuality, like Sengle's as an autonomous symbolic formation. Messalina suffers from the unending displacement of such a symbolically formed "object." She must, but cannot, halt desire in order to terminate the object's lunatic flight.[28]

The structure of *Messalina,* characteristic of Jarry's fiction, foreshadows modern novels. It may be interpreted, in light of Freudian theory, as a derivation of primary erotogenic masochism. Sexual activity is everywhere, in Jarry's anticipatory texts, inscribed in the dual aim of desire and death. Brazenly exceeding known limits has no goal but an inherent violent and fatal outcome. Desire, to exist, demands continued deferral. Fulfillment, or presence, heralds pain and death. Like Freud, Jarry examined the connections among erotic pleasure, pain, and death in aggression: between partners and self-inflicted.[29] For Jarry, love and sex harbor an ironic nihilism, that is, a virulent alliance of love and humor, generating the "corrosive" quality of modern narrative: at its best, it is ferocious, sharp-shooting, and acidic.

All of Jarry's characters function in texts which privilege their autonomy and the juxtaposition of images, events, and theories. Modern too on the level of expression and typography, the novels combine conflicting modes and styles of writing, including scientific jargon, philosophical "essays," dialogue (usually indicating delirium, hallucination, or intoxication), musical and mathematical notation, seals, epigraphs, dedications, isolated words, lists, and documents (to serve a narrative function). Italics, blank spaces, capital letters, and Jarry's own masterful woodcuts are used with dramatic effect.

Jarry's experiments with type and layout increase textual difficulty, a phenomenon that has become a hallmark of complex, obscure, resistant modernist narrative. "Difficult" texts are commonly called "unreadable," in the sense that they are "corrosive" vis-à-vis all institutionalized values. An unreadable text disconcerts by its absolute opacity or excessive transparency. Often, it distorts and contradicts itself by playing with levels of denotation and connotation. Anti-Aristotelian and blasphemous, spatial and schizoform, the modernist novel (in the lineage of Sade, Raymond Roussel, Joyce, or Philippe Sollers) thus enacts its own alienation. The difficult, unreadable text subverts and confuses (disorients and mixes up) by contradicting hierarchy and finite polarities. Its theatrical, heraldic discourse dissimulates and sets traps, titillates and insults.

Typically, *Faustroll* opens with an official order to pay the rent, written in "legalese." Sengle, in turn, receives the Lieutenant's "prose piece" and a letter requesting him to submit this story to a magazine. This technique aims, with irony and caustic humor, at helping the reader "believe" and offers yet another point of view.

Juxtaposition, then, does not—as it sometimes seems—create or reproduce chaos, but better presents and redefines reality, by including all its contradictory, complementary, and fragmented elements. To this end, modern novelists insist on including all facets of reality, be they irrational or bizarre, horrifying or ambiguous. In the same manner as cinematographic montage, the modern novel organizes disparate and discontinuous components which the perceiving mind must interpret. The novel's "meaning" derives from the rapport or "collision" among juxtaposed units.

Sequence and progression may be further subverted by stressing the exceptional, the unexpected, or the easily ignored features of the hero's world. One approach exploits the camera's "close-up" shot: Faustroll, in one experiment, is miniaturized, with the result that a cabbage leaf and water droplets upon it are greatly enlarged. Not only does this afford an unusual perspective, but, in effect, this "close-up" suspends time. Indeed, when defining "pataphysics" Jarry emphasizes that his science will study the specific; it addresses laws which govern exceptions.[30] In Jarry's novels, viewing the exceptional or the particular frequently takes the form of a timeless gaze into the subject's eyes. Faustroll explicitly invokes the art of the camera to explain this spatialized "gap" in time: "A good watch [. . .] would have cost me an excessive sum, and then, I do not engage in secular experiences, I do not take continuity seriously, and I judge it more aesthetic to keep Time itself in a pocket, or the temporal unit, which is the snapshot."[31]

Suspending time in favor of space creates a powerful, expansive present. This is precisely the significance of Jarry's "ethernity." A character may travel into the past or the future, or both simultaneously. The conclusion of "Commentary to Help in the Practical Construction of the Time-Machine" states: *"Duration is the transformation of succession into a reversal.* That is to say: THE BECOMING OF A MEMORY."[32] Because of this same kind of destruction of linear time and because of the theoretically mobile structure of juxtaposition, certain modern novels give the impression of circular motion. Faustroll's journey from Paris to Paris and his repeatedly mentioned circular flow of blood offer overt representations of such movement. The Doctor explicitly describes luminiferous ether (the medium through which he travels after his death) as *"circular, mobile,* and perishable."[33] More symbolic, however, is the gyrostat (gyroscope in a case) used to navigate the Time-Machine, and adopted by a considerable number of modern novelists as a structural model.

An important model of modern novels—and one especially pertinent to Jarry's fiction—organizes space in binary relations. The negative and the positive, given basic mathematical form in the play *Caesar-Antichrist,* parallel the doubles who people the novels, the dominant spatial configurations, and the repeated images (such as heads detached from bodies). The novels construct a dialectical scaffolding, however, only to raze it by denying the existence of opposites. Jarry selects a deliberately limited system in which sets of images and words are constantly recombined: that system is Pataphysics. Its tenets are utterly arbitrary but once set in motion it builds a coherent, complex edifice. This approximates the functioning of the "closed field" in mathematics.[34] Within Jarry's "closed field" there is no sign, though, of claustral fantasy. For just as scientists discovered that matter, when disintegrated, yields energy and is not, in fact, unchangeable, Jarry, by decomposing his psyche (splitting and reduplicating his ego) and by applying the concepts of relativity, system, dialectical synthesis, and superimposition to his writing, displays in his novels a great release of energy, what Nin termed "the intense activity of an inner drama."[35]

Jarry's narration of that drama evolved from his intuition of modern consciousness. Writing at a critical moment in the history of men and letters, he intuited and established a new sensibility and a new dialect. His example of fragmentation, madness, eroticism, and "unreadability" reverberates through modern narrative. The seeds of modernity were sown not only in Le Père Ubu's conscious iconoclasm, but in Jarry's *self-conscious* prose.

Chapter Seven
Conclusion

In 1979, Tvetan Todorov (quoting Roland Barthes) wrote: "The individual is no longer an essence, as was the case in what is now for us a mythical, classical past. But neither is he a Romantic fusion of opposites, the noble criminal, the passionate rationalist—in other words, a living oxymoron; today, the self is viewed as 'a diffraction, a dispersion leaving in its wake neither a central nucleus, nor any meaningful structure; the 'I' is not merely contradictory: it is dispersed.' "[1] Todorov suggests that the modernity of literature which takes this phenomenon into account lies in its perception of the contemporary era as one of "generalized alterity and exteriorization," and of "a new feeling of inner multiplicity." "Perhaps," he concludes, "it is through literature that one can read most clearly the characteristics of our time."[2] Leo Bersani, in his 1977 *Baudelaire and Freud,* asserts that modern writing rejects the idealist dualism of the Romantic vision (which nonetheless accepts the possibility of wholeness and presence) in favor of exocentric fragments of the Self (which being in essence marginal "resist all efforts to make a unifying structure of fragmented desire"). Consequently, the images of a "disseminated, scattered self" harbor in turn unmoored "shifting centers."[3]

In light of this critical collage, it is no accident that mirroring, doubling, repetition, and displacement inform Jarry's novels, taken individually or intertexually. A decentered pluralism of psychic self-theatricalizations has become the hallmark of the modern psyche. With the help of psychoanalytic discourse Jarry's texts become clearly intelligible and they are eerily predictive of modern consciousness. Psychoanalysis explains the symbolic relations which structure the Subject; and the dominant "psychological disposition" of modern Western culture—according to social historian Christopher Lasch and analysts Otto Kernberg and Heinz Kohut—is narcissism. Jarry's self-theatricalization into a multiplicity of doubles tragically renders material a madness which marks the particular pathology of the modern era.

Narcissism, in its various manifestations throughout Jarry's texts, exceeds mere rhetorical posturing around the image of self-engrossment or of the infolding of language itself. His writings concretize, with astonishing lucidity, the delirious fragmentation of man and, correlatively, of his discourse. The essential fragmentation of this textual universe, however, in Jarry's case, mimes what was probably the primal splitting of pathological narcissism.[4] The most insistent narrative patterns and dramatic characterizations in the fiction trace biographemes such as the absent father, the mother's devaluation of the father, and the exaggerated role of the son in the mother's defense system. Add to these the probability of guilt regarding the death of his infant brother. His avowed need to be special, unique, or, to quote him, "precious," acts as a nodal point for a range of isolating and terrifying narcissistic fantasies. Perpetual-Motion-Food nourishes a pathologically grandiose self and assures its omnipotence. The economy of grandiosity that makes these fantasies manifest themselves accounts, for example, for the she-dragoon's characteristics of being "precious and double." This severe narcissistic disturbance is exemplified by Sengle's pathological identification with a love object standing for his past self, and his withdrawal into "splendid isolation," achieving "anxiety tolerance" by increasing his narcissistic fantasies. Marcueil's narcissistic personality is in part distinguished by his charming facade behind which lurk coldness and ruthlessness. The Supermale's sexual and athletic exploits, because of their very automatism and absence of pleasure, aim at neutralizing or forestalling the chronic threat of fragmentation that precedes the full-blown psychosis. Marcueil typifies the narcissistic male: his arrogant and exploitive behavior toward women derives from an unconscious projection of hostility against the imago of the mother.

Obsessively freighted with metaphors of the Double, seemingly endless stratification of perverse sexual penchants, and reliance on "primary process" thinking (rejecting linear causality in favor of symbolism and magic), works such as *Days and Nights* and *The Supermale* afford Jarry the therapeutic opportunity to act out the pathological characterology with which he invests his literary counterparts. He projected his intrapsychic aggression and anxiety upon incarnations of his fundamental personality organization. This tendency to "primitivize" thought leads from Ubu's stilted diction to the obsessional use of neologisms. Symptomatic of the narcissist's inner void, "Ubu-speak" is the diction of a robot, never sincerely jealous, sad, angry, and who cannot cry. Ubu transposes this personality in yet another way: "People may appear [to the narcissist] either to have some potential food inside, which the patient has to extract, or to be already emptied and therefore valueless. His attitude toward others is either deprecatory—he has extracted all he needs and tosses them aside—or fearful—others may attack, exploit, and force him to submit to them." His greed, destructiveness, and intense ambition are all characteristic of the narcissist. Likewise, Sengle's antisocial behavior, Haldern's sadistic and open physical violence toward the object of his sexual exploits, and Emmanuel God's "self-concept of the hungry wolf." Emmanuel God's oral-sadistic fantasy relates to his identification of his eyes with sharp-fanged wolves. Generally, the most basic mother-infant interactions reside in the domain of the visual. Often aggressively cathected, the visual takes the place of failed physical contact (oral or tactile) or even of the mother's closeness. Narcissism goes hand in hand with a hypercathected visual sense, as Faustroll's visit to the Isle of Her illustrates. There, the water's immobile surface is "like a mirror" and its sovereign is a Cyclops. In front of this giant male's frontal eye hangs a two-sided mirror. His extraordinary sight easily penetrates ultraviolet "things." This therapeutic activation of the grandiose self corresponds to Kohut's "mirror transference" in which the child seeks to retain a degree of archaic narcissism, on the one hand, by attributing perfection and strength to a grandiose self and, on the other hand, by relegating all imperfection to the external world. The narcissist attempts to reestablish the stage when the mother's gaze—reflecting the child's exhibitionism or other aspects of maternal participation in her child's narcissistic pleasure—confirms the individual's self-esteem.

The abnormal narcissist cannot integrate "good and bad self-images into a realistic self-concept that incorporates rather than dissociates the various component self representations."[5] Nor can he sustain interaction between the self and the other. Such incapacity to coordinate or to differentiate the self from the other reflects a basic insecurity of object-relations. Regression to moments of pathogenic fixation blurs the boundaries among impulse, thought, and action. The chapter "Pataphysique" in *Days and Nights* foresees ego psychology when it perfects the "leibnizian definition": Sengle "did not at all distinguish his thoughts from his acts nor his dreams from his waking state." The deserter was accustomed to directing "Things" by thought alone (794). A typical narcissistic patient of Kohut's told of childhood fantasies in which he controlled a trolley by thought waves emanating from his head as it flew above the clouds. The detached head is also, of course, Sengle's emblem extraordinary. Likewise, the idealized parental image must be maintained in its archaic form in order to maintain narcissistic homeostasis. The image is not transformed and internalized as a part of the individual's psychic structure.

In "The Mirror-Stage" ("Le stade du miroir comme formateur de la fonction du Je") Jacques Lacan stresses the connection between two forces: the aggression exhibited by the narcissistic libido in its relationships with others (even when such aggression is masked by seeming "samaratanism") is closely linked to the alienating function of the self as subject.[6] The mirror stage is a stage in development when the subject splits in order to see itself simultaneously as ego and as "other," as presence and as absence. The reflection in the mirror, paradoxically self and other/image, alienates the self from itself. As Jarry's texts (especially *The Supermale*) demonstrate, narcissistic sexual desire—to take one example of the dynamics of this division—is fundamentally masochistic: "the subject fantasizes an ecstatic death as the result of being attacked by an alien self"[7] (cf. the Love-Inspiring Machine animated by Marcueil's own strength). An equally sumptuous occurrence of autoerotic activity portrays Sengle kissing the lips of Valens: "The plaster mouth became flesh and red in order to drink the libation of Sengle's soul [. . .]. And after the instant of redness, the lips turned green and adhered, completely cold, to Sengle's blackened lips" (835). This reverse alchemical symbolism (proceeding from red to green to black) mimics the narcissistic regression at work in the novel.

Jarry evokes a similar image when he declares his wish to be so hideous that his presence would cause women to abort in the streets or give birth to Siamese twins joined at the forehead. Such desires betoken the symptoms of narcissistic rage that permeate his life and his art. Often, the precariously omnipotent characters swing from experiences of inner devastation to grandiose potentiality and infinite freedom. Their need for homage and adoration (in the cases of, for example, Haldern and Emmanuel God), their exploitive and at times parasitic relationships with others (Ubu above all), give rise to defensive fantasies of grandeur[8] and inflated self-concepts, evidence of developmental arrest.

The motif of oral-aggressive conflicts throughout Jarry's works symbolizes the "hungry infant" hiding behind "narcissistic armour." Pertinent manifestations of oral hostility, typical of narcissistic personality disorders, portray Emmanuel God as the "hungry wolf," Lucien biting the "shark" on the mouth, Ubu's insatiable and cruelly imposed appetite, the bite of embryos on the Amorphic Isle visited by Faustroll and that of the dagger suffered by Messalina, or the burning bite (compared to being cut by a saw) that causes even Ellen Elson to faint. This motif's apotheosis features the "incandescent jaw" of the "electro-loving" machine electrocuting Marcueil. Because of the economically reversed countercathexis of libidinal energy, the machine sinks its white-hot teeth in the Supermale's head. The boomerang of energy generated by his own drives fatally gratifies the narcissistic self that takes itself as its object of desire. In *The She-Dragoon* dental aggression literally becomes the novel's battleground, for it is in the town of Morsang that dragoons clash: the weapons as well as our hero and heroine. Morsang, likened to a gaping jaw, joins (as do the Siamese twins Jarry would have liked to conjure) two key signifiers: *morsure* ("bite") and *sang* ("blood").

Rather than "repression, the primary active defense against anxiety" for the normal adult, the narcissist continues to use "primitive splitting" as first experienced in the infantile mirror-stage. Narcissistic splitting structures the texts in various ways, from the doubles who inhabit them to the pataphysical message that opposites are equal, but it is best iconized by the intersecting oblique lines of the letter X. Architectural image and alphabetical symbol, X is a facade, simultaneously an inscription and a fiction. Algebraic notation and clinical (psychoanalytic) sign, X designates the unknown quantity and makes visible the unconscious's language. Importantly, the X appears in *Caesar-Antichrist* as the *bâton-à-physique* rotating on its axis and as the cross; in *Absolute Love* it is Xavier's deconstructed and deconstructive initial as well as the crossbones of death. In *The She-Dragoon*, X becomes the trope and the tropism of crossed swords (in the duel) in addition to being the insignia of the couple Erbrand and Jeanne. It is implicit in the figure of the dual-sexed androgyn or hermaphrodite (also symbolized by the *bâton*) and thereby evokes the unconscious image of the phallic mother who reigns during the pre-Oedipal, oral stage of narcissism. In *The Supermale,* as in science, X signifies simply the "unexpected force" (101). Most frequently, the letter/grapheme has a properly semiotic function: it signifies death (as in the Xavier episode), desire, and the phallus. Haldern would have his lover Ablou carve an X on his palm as proof of their "brotherly" love. The duke thus implores his page in his efforts to win a kiss. Instead, Haldern kisses Ablou and there follows talk of bloody swords sadistically copulating. Haldern then leaves behind a pensive Ablou, who images his lord (potentially scarred by the X) as a bounding phallus (220).

As opposed to integration of the superego (a restricting agency which prohibits) and the ego ideal (a gratifying agency which serves wish fulfillment), the narcissist polarizes and separates segments of his experience.[9] *Absolute Love* illustrates this disintegration by placing Emmanuel God in a prison cell where he is constantly observed by images of his own superego. The narcissist retains an idealized parental imago in its archaic form, activated, as in the case of Emmanuel God's "true" Virgin Mother, to balance narcissistic rage. Nor can he integrate "good" and "bad" parental images. The image of his mother, dominating the novel, shifts from vamp to vampire to virgin: a classic Madonna/whore syndrome. Unable, like his fellow heroes, to establish profound and enduring rapports—love and friendship fail; marriage is never considered—his relationships become combative, warlike, and barbaric, aping modern social life.[10]

Instead of sublimating (or repressing) conflicts in a socially acceptable manner, Jarry's characters typically "act out" their psychic battles. Although, as Kernberg asserts, the narcissist often has a capacity for pseudosublimation (that is, he may seemingly function well in his work and may in fact be extremely creative), he "often thinks of himself as an outlaw and sees others in the same way, as basically dishonest and unreliable." Faustroll skips town when the bailiff appears, Sengle feigns illness to evade the army, Ubu and Emmanuel God end up in prison, Marc-Pol is hanged by the Sheik, and Haldern commits homicide to destroy the evidence of his sexual aggression and to halt the narcissistic seesaw movement in which he and his servant exchange roles—in other words, to escape his interminable otherness. The "cult of sensuality [so prevalent in modern society and illustrated in *The Supermale,* subtitled *modern novel*] implies a repudiation of sensuality in all but its most primitive forms."

In retrospect, Jarry's writings seem to express particularly well the pathology which governs the fundamental personality configuration of the modern age. Christopher Lasch offers a Marxian comparison of this phenomenon to times past: "In Freud's time, hysteria and obsessional neurosis carried to extremes the personality traits associated with the capitalist order at an earlier stage in its development—acquisitiveness, fanatical, devotion to work, and a fierce repression of sexuality." Today, society is characterized by "the social emphasis on consumption rather than the production of commodities, the rise of the mass media with their cult of glamor and celebrity, the disruption of the sense of historical continuity."[11] In other words, modern social structures, which both reflect and cause particular personality contours, are apt to foster "narcissistic" patterns of behaviors and beliefs. The relationship between the Self and the Other is modified by structures of alienation, such as division of labor into mutually exclusive social contexts and performances. This combines adversely with the dismantling of those cultural standards which allow the Self to situate itself in realistically perceived time and space. A narcissistic identity develops when cultural norms and social structures no longer permit the Self to integrate realistically into the process of production. This type of imbalance in real and imaginary relations between the Self and the Other is conducive to the glorification of the "Me."

Heinz Kohut compares Freud's clientele—suffering from *unresolved* Oedipal conflicts resulting from the pressures of Victorian family life—to contemporary psychiatric patients whose disorders issue from the *absence* of normal Oedipal conflicts.[12] This phenomenon may produce an insensitive, lonely, emotionally understimulated adult lacking social responsibility and moral conscience. Because of his subsequent need for narcissistic gratification, such a person runs the psychogenic risk of becoming drug-addicted, alcoholic, perverted, or obese. Drugs, alcohol, sexual perversion, and obesity are self-evident in Jarry's opus. The grandiose self "feeds" itself in self-defense against a world perceived as hostile, frustrating, and unsatisfying. This self obsessively needs admiration and superego values that were not internalized at a phase-appropriate time. During the stage of Freudian "primary narcissism," approximating Jacques Lacan's "mirror-stage," the infant does not distinguish between his own specular image and the reflection of his mother holding him up to the mirror. The mirror is, of course, a metaphor for both the mother's gaze which returns his own image to the infant and the perception of another human. The passage from the image-stage of dual relation with the Mother (Lacan's "Imaginary Order") to socially mediated relationships of the language-stage (Lacan's "Symbolic Order") requires a completion of the Oedipalization process signaling the end of dependency on the Mother. Because of many factors, including today's commonly loose-knit family structure often marked by absentee parents, this process does not necessarily occur.

Thus, the subject is denied what Julia Kristeva calls the confrontation of the Imaginary and the Symbolic which subverts domination and "dissolves narcissistic fixations."[13] The infant would in this way escape total absorption by either parent, the Father (Symbolic, language) or the Mother (Imaginary, image). This is one of the reasons the narcissist is incapable of true love: according to Lacan, love functions at the crossroads of these two orders.[14] Instead of loving, the narcissist seeks mirrors of admiration. Trapped in a world of alienating images of the ego, in which the mother-child relationship or the mother figure pervades the subject's thoughts—*Absolute Love* is the apotheosis of this disorder of the self—the subject operates in a realm of resemblances, where meaning is based on identity (rather than difference) and where the structures of vision predominate:[15] witness Jarry's thesis of the identity of opposites and his obsession with the power of the eye (of sight and of clairvoyance). A critic affirmed in 1980 that "to study the Imaginary is to engage in a kind of 'pataphysics.' "[16] The modern age has produced a literature of the Imaginary that enciphers resemblances and portrays the embodiment of primitive resemblances: the madman.[17] Faustroll, the supreme pataphysician, is not the only one of Jarry's characters gripped by psychotic episodes.

A fictional character such as this is "mad," however, in more than the conventional sense of the term. Michel Foucault delineates the madman as "the man of primitive resemblances [. . .] who is *alienated in analogy*. [. . .] He inverts all values and all proportions . . . for him, the crown makes the king." Inversely, he calls the "age of resemblance" one of "madness and imagination." "Resemblance" is further identified as "the invisible form of that which . . . made things visible." The visible figure necessary to reveal this form is, according to Foucault, "hieroglyphics," a category including blazons, ciphers, and obscure words. Many aspects of Jarry's aesthetics correspond to these hypotheses. The narcissistic paradox of dichotomy in Sameness is perhaps the most striking. His insistent use of heraldry, codewords, neologisms, musical and mathematical signs, and cryptic intertextual references all mark his writing as participating in Madness and the Imaginary.

Recurrent images of decapitation and castration and the constant anxiety that accompanies them illustrate the pathologically narcissistic fantasy of the body's being cut into pieces. Repetitive mention of knives, swords, daggers, and other trenchant objects embellishes the fantasy and explicitly links the fear of dismemberment to desire. Paradoxically, the anguish precipitated by the fragmentation of the body-image also becomes, in the texts, a spatial void concretized by hollow forms or unfathomable emptiness. Typical of narcissistic fantasies, the cutting of the body and the implicit image of separation combine with the characters' narcissistic object-choice, that is, the desired object represents some aspect of the character's own self: his love is directed toward his own image. The textual cipher of the letter X unifies a narcissistic object-choice, the flesh under the knife, and the abyss (or death). X—letter of the unconscious and sign of superficially "unreadable" narcissism—is the signature that assures the circulation of currency of the individual who has not developed beyond the "oral stage" of narcissistic reflections.

One particularly apt Foucaldian description of the modern age sums up Jarry's personal torment and his textual system, both of which are characterized by narcissism and alienation: "the identity of the return of the Same with the absolute dispersion of man."[18]

Notes and References

Chapter One

1. See Chapter 2 for an explanation of this concept, one central to Jarry's theory of Pataphysics. For Jarry, "simplicity" is "condensed complexity."

2. Rachilde (pseud.), *Alfred Jarry; ou le Surmâle des lettres* (Paris, 1928), p. 31. This translation, and all translations throughout the text, are my own, unless otherwise indicated.

3. Paul Chauveau, *Alfred Jarry, ou la naissance, la vie et la mort du Père Ubu, avec leurs portraits* (Paris, 1932), p. 50.

4. Henri de Régnier, *De Mon temps* (Paris: Mercure de France, 1933), p. 150.

5. Ibid., p. 153.

6. Noël Arnaud, *Alfred Jarry, d'Ubu roi au Docteur Faustroll* (Paris, 1974), p. 95. Arnaud offers the testimony of Georges Rémond, Octave Fluchaire, and Sosthène Morand.

7. This title cannot be definitively translated because of the triple meaning of *sable:* the animal, the heraldic color, and sand.

8. Arnaud, *Jarry,* p. 122.

9. Roger Shattuck, *The Banquet Years* (New York, 1955), pp. 211–12.

10. André Salmon, *Souvenirs sans fin* (Paris: Gallimard, 1955), p. 151.

11. Rachilde, *Jarry,* p. 181.

12. Shattuck, *Banquet,* p. 191.

13. Guillaume Apollinaire, *Il y a* (Paris: Messein, 1925), p. 173.

14. Rachilde, *Jarry,* p. 175.

15. J. H. Lévesque, *Alfred Jarry* (Paris, 1951), p. 92.

16. Rachilde, *Jarry,* p. 164.

17. Alfred Jarry, *Oeuvres complètes,* presented and annotated by Michel Arrivé, Bibliothèque de la Pléiade (Paris, 1972), 1:1238. Hereafter, page numbers inserted parenthetically in the text refer to this edition.

18. Again, an untranslatable title: *le moutardier* is a mustard maker, but the expression "Il se croit le premier moutardier du pape" (He

thinks he is the Pope's chief mustard maker) means: "He's not half proud of himself."

19. Published in 1943; edited by Jean Saltas, whose pen probably finished the text.

20. Rachilde, *Jarry*, p. 223.

Chapter Two

1. In "Puppet Show": a protomorphic version of *Ubu Cuckolded*, published 28 April 1893, in *L'Echo de Paris mensuel illustré* and incorporated into *Les Minutes de sable mémorial*, published in 1894.

2. Roger Shattuck, "What is Pataphysics?" *Evergreen Review* 4, no. 13 (May-June 1960):25.

3. François Caradec, "Rabelais dans l'oeuvre de Jarry," *Cahiers du Collège de Pataphysique*, no. 15 (23 clinamen 81), pp. 43–48.

4. Described in Charles Vernon Boys's *Soap Bubbles, Their Colours and the Forces Which Mould Them* (New York: The Macmillan Co., 1920).

5. Gilbert Durand, *Structures anthropologiques de l'imaginaire* (Paris: Bordas, 1969), p. 141.

6. Ibid., p. 89.

7. Carl Jung, *Psyche and Symbol* (New York: Doubleday Anchor Books, 1958), pp. 113–47.

8. See Michel Arrivé, *Les langages de Jarry* (Paris, 1972), pp. 121–52, for a detailed exposition of the sexual connotation of this and other symbols in *Caesar-Antichrist*.

9. François Caradec places Jarry's description of death in the Celtic, rather than the Judeo-Latin or Christian traditions. See his *A la Recherche d'Alfred Jarry* (Paris, 1974), p. 33.

10. André Breton, *Anthologie de l'humour noir* (Paris: Jean-Jacques Pauvert, 1966), pp. 272–73.

11. Ruy Launoir mentions Heisenberg in the context of Pataphysics in *Clefs pour la Pataphysique* (Paris: Seghers, 1969), p. 38.

12. Walter Sullivan, "A Hole in the Sky," *New York Times Magazine*, 14 July 1974, p. 11.

13. Ibid., pp. 11, 34–35.

14. H. G. Wells's science fiction novel *The Time Machine* had just been translated, by Davray, into French. Jarry's text appeared—with Faustroll's signature!—in February 1899 in the *Mercure de France*, no. 110, pp. 387–96.

15. Sullivan, "A Hole in the Sky," p. 34.

16. Ibid., pp. 34–35.

17. Ibid., p. 34.

18. Gayatri Spivak and Michael Ryan, "Anarchism Rivisited: A New Philosophy," *Diacritics,* Summer 1978, p. 75.

19. Jacques Derrida, tr. Gayatri Spivak, *Of Grammatology* (Baltimore: Johns Hopkins University Press, 1974), Translator's preface, p. lix.

20. Jacques Derrida, "La Différance," in *Tel Quel: Théorie d'ensemble* (Paris: Seuil, 1968), p. 48.

21. Jacques Derrida, *Positions* (Paris: Les Editions de Minuit, 1972), p. 41.

22. Spivak, "Anarchism Revisited," p. 75.

23. James H. Bierman, "A Reader's Guide to *César-Antechrist:* A Fresh Look at the Theater of Alfred Jarry" (Ph.D. dissertation, Stanford University, 1968), note, p. 6.

24. For a detailed list of the founders and Statutes, as well as descriptions of the first meeting and the contents of each publication, see Lewis F. Sutton, "An Evaluation of the Studies on Alfred Jarry from 1894–1963" (Ph.D. Dissertation, University of North Carolina at Chapel Hill, 1966), pp. 139–55.

25. The first issue appeared on 6 April 1950, or 15 clinamen 77 E.P.

Chapter Three

1. *Ubu roi, Ubu cocu, Ubu enchaîné, Ubu sur la Butte,* "L'Acte Terrestre" of *César-Antechrist,* "Chez Madame Ubu" of *L'Amour en visites,* and "L'Art et la Science," which is Part III of "Guignol" of *Les Minutes de sable mémorial.*

2. Roger Bensky, *Structures textuelles de la marionnette de langue française* (Paris: Nizet, 1969), p. 52.

3. Micheline Tison-Braun, *La Crise de l'humanisme* (Paris: Nizet, 1958–67), 1:90.

4. Arrivé, *Les langages de Jarry,* p. 315.

5. Antonin Artaud, *The Theater and Its Double,* tr. Mary Caroline Richards (New York: Grove Press, 1958), p. 44.

6. J. E. Cirlot, *A Dictionary of Symbols,* tr. Jack Sage (New York: Philosophical Library, 1962), p. 290.

7. Ibid., pp. 291–92.

8. It is formed by intercallating an "r" into the vulgar but "real" word *merde.*

9. "Mère Ubu: What! You say nothing, Père Ubu. Have you forgotten the word then?

Père Ubu: Mère . . . Ubu! I don't want to utter the word anymore, it cost me too much unpleasantness" (429). In fact, *merdre* turns up disguised as a play on *armée*, rendered *armerdre*.

10. Hunter Kevil, *"Les Minutes de sable mémorial* by Alfred Jarry" (Ph.D. dissertation, Princeton University, 1975), pp. 297–98.

11. Roger Bensky, *Recherches sur les structures et la symbolique de la marionnette* (Paris: Nizet, 1971).

12. Bensky, *Structures textuelles,* p. 52.

13. *La chandelle verte,* Edition établie et présentée par Maurice Saillet (Paris: Livre de Poche, 1969), p. 630.

14. Henri Bergson, *Le Rire, essai sur la signification du comique* (Paris: Presses Universitaires de France, 1940), p. 101.

15. *La chandelle verte,* p. 70.

16. Ibid., p. 35. In France, stamps can be purchased in a "tobacco shop."

17. Ibid., pp. 59–60.

18. Francis Carco, "Reflexions sur l'humour," *Mercure de France* 110, no. 409 (1 July 1914):56.

19. Breton devotes a chapter of his *Anthologie de l'humour noir* to Jarry (Paris: Jean-Jacques Pauvert, 1966).

20. Philippe Soupault, "Confrontations Alfred Jarry," *Cahiers de la Compagnie Renaud-Barrault,* nos. 22–23 (May 1958), p. 176.

21. Breton, *Anthologie,* p. 273.

22. Ibid., p. 15.

23. Sigmund Freud, *Jokes and Their Relation to the Unconscious,* tr. James Strachey (New York: Norton, 1960), p. 105.

24. "Ames solitaires," a critique of Gerhart Hauptmann's *Einsame Menschen,* published in *L'Art litteraire,* nos. 1–2 (jan.-fév. 1894), pp. 21–25.

25. The translation of the title is Roger Bensky's.

26. Anne Clancier, *Psychanalyse et critique littéraire* (Toulouse: Nouvelles Recherches/PRIVAT, 1973), p. 12.

27. Ibid., p. 79.

28. Ibid.

29. Cirlot, *Dictionary,* pp. 81–84.

Chapter Four

1. First published in the *Mercure de France*, July 1894.
2. J.-H. Sainmont, "Déchiffrement d'un fragment inédit d'Alfred Jarry concernant *Les Jours et les Nuits*," *Dossiers du Collège de 'Pataphysique*, 22 Merdre XCI E.P., pp. 8–9.
3. Artaud, *The Theater and Its Double*, pp. 101–2.
4. Arnaud, *Jarry*, p. 98.
5. Maurice Blanchot, *Lautréamont et Sade* (Paris: Editions de Minuit, 1963), pp. 96, 137.
6. Ibid., p. 181.
7 Completed in 1845 and invoked as well by Baudelaire in *Paradis artificiels*.
8. The "inorganic siren" refers to the music of the phonograph in "Phonographe," a work in *Les Minutes*. The image of a decapitated being—indicating the Double—is also central to "Phonographe": "They took my head, my head—And put it in a tea-caddy!" (p. 186). The phonograph will also figure importantly in *The Supermale*.
9. Jarry served in the 101st regiment of the infantry, whose ranks he joined on 13 November 1894 (Arnaud, *Jarry*, p. 135). Happily, his stint was cut short (Arnaud, *Jarry*, p. 349).
10. The physical body is the product and the support of the other components; the astral body unites the inferior physical element to the superior spiritual element and is doubly polarized; the immortal Spirit is the third constituent. Dr. G. Encausse Papus, *Qu'est-ce que l'occultisme?* (Paris: Editions Niclaus, 1951), p. 18.
11. Jarry had already described the split between the astral and the terrestrial bodies in "Opium," part of *Les Minutes:* "And my astral body, kicking my terrestrial body with its heel, left like a pilgrim, leaving a quivering of guitar strings in my nerves" (p. 195); and he would again in *The Other Alceste*, where the astral body served as a monstrous ferryman who transported a soul in a green silk envelope through the marshlands (p. 910).
12. Arnaud, *Jarry*, p. 364.
13. Durand, *Structures*, pp. 145, 147.
14. J. Chasseguet-Smirgel, "Du stade anal dans la formation de l'image du corps," paper presented to the Société psychanalytique de Paris, 1959. Cited in Clancier, *Psychanalyse*, pp. 92–93.
15. Micromegas is a character in a philosophical short story by Voltaire (1752). He lands on Saturn and, accompanied by a Saturnian, visits Earth. Micromegas may have especially appealed to Jarry because

of his Saturnian association. Saturn symbolizes "the necessity for the 'reign of Cronos' to be succeeded by another cosmic mode of existence in which time has no place." Cirlot, *Dictionary,* p. 265.

16. Ibid., p. 111. The following treatment of the myth is based on ibid., pp. 111–12.

17. Ibid., p. 137.

18. Ibid., pp. 111–12.

19. Otto Rank, *The Double,* tr. Harry Tucker (Chapel Hill: University of North Carolina Press, 1971), pp. 73, 83.

20. André Green, *The Tragic Effect,* tr. Alan Sheridan (Cambridge: Cambridge University Press, 1979), p. 237.

21. Otto Rank, *The Double,* pp. 74, 80, 86.

22. Ibid., p. 75.

23. Ibid., pp. 77, 79.

24. Ibid., p. 67.

25. Jean Gillibert, "Le travestissement: Jean Genêt," paper presented to the Société psychanalytique de Paris, cited in Clancier, *Psychanalyse,* p. 76.

26. Louis Lormel tells of Jarry's incongruous discourse praising masturbation, during a café meeting of writers and publishers. Fargue, his constant companion, added, "First of all, what is Art if not intellectual masturbation?" "Entre Soi," *La Plume,* no. 203 (1er octobre 1897), p. 606. It is possible that Jarry's homosexual experimentation was part of his program to "create" himself, and that he was motivated by literary reasons.

27. Rachilde reports Jarry's opinion that women have no souls in *Jarry,* p. 33.

28. The gnostic Helen was imagined by Simon the Magus. Hippolyte of Rome described his doctrine in his *Philosophumena.*

29. Arnaud, *Jarry,* p. 234.

30. This article first appeared in *L'Art littéraire,* nouvelle série, nos. 5–6 (mai-juin 1894), pp. 77–82.

31. Gaston Bachelard, *L'Air et les songes* (Paris: José Corti, 1943), p. 33.

32. *Oeuvres complètes* (Lausanne et Monte Carlo: Henri Kaeser, 1948), 3:153.

33. This complex of images appears as well in *Absolute Love,* p. 952.

34. Jung explains that primitive, or prerational, man believes that by donning the mask of his "bush soul" he literally becomes the Other being. For example, a witch doctor wearing a lion mask is not pretending to be a lion; he believes he *is* a lion. "He shares a 'psychic

identity' with the animal." *Man and His Symbols* (Garden City, N.Y.: Doubleday, 1972), p. 45. Jung writes of a "Burmese buffalo dance in which masked dancers are possessed by the buffalo spirit" (p. 236).

35. "Time homosexually copulates with my Hours using his black pentagonal escutcheon, a shovel, whose Triangle emerges, thrust in."

36. *La chandelle verte,* Edition établie et présentée par Maurice Saillet (Paris: Livre de Poche, 1969), p. 168.

Chapter Five

1. Green, *Tragic,* p. 133.

2. Ibid., pp. 35–87: "Orestes and Oedipus: From the Oracle to the Law."

3. Ibid., pp. 43, 47.

4. Ibid., p. 55.

5. Ibid., p. 86.

6. Ibid., p. 57.

7. S. Freud, *Standard Edition of the Complete Psycho-logical Works,* (London: Hogarth Press, 1953–66), 18:273.

8. M. Scriabine, cited in Green, *Tragic,* p. 254.

9. Ibid., p. 65.

10. *Oeuvres complètes d'Alfred Jarry* (Lausanne, Monte Carlo: Henri Kaeser, 1948), 3:117. Page numbers in parentheses in this section refer to this edition.

11. For the symbolism of the "shadow" see Chapter 4.

12. *La Chandelle verte,* p. 171.

13. *Oeuvres complètes,* Pléiade edition, p. 876.

14. *Oeuvres complètes,* Monte Carlo edition, p. 110.

15. Their impact was immediately recognized by Apollinaire and Salmon, who printed an excerpt of *The Beloved Object* in *Le Festin d'Europe* in November 1903, and by Marinetti, who, in 1908, printed the complete text in *Poesia* (Caradec, *A la Recherche d'Alfred Jarry,* p. 122).

16. In *La Plume* 1903: "Le mimétisme inverse chez les personnages de Henri de Regnier."

17. This episode transcribes the attempted seduction of Jarry by Berthe de Courrière, mistress of his friend Rémy de Gourmont. The lubricious lady is bitterly depicted as a vulgar sorceress.

18. For a detailed analysis of each tableau in this novel, see my "L'Amour polymorphe d'Alfred Jarry," *Nineteenth Century French Studies,* Fall/Winter 1979–80.

19. "Masculinity 'has nothing to do with biological sexuality but with the patriarchal and symbolic order,' " says Michèle Blin-Sarde, in "L'Evolution du Concept de Différence dans le Mouvement de Libération des Femmes en France," *Journal of Contemporary French Civilization*, Spring 1981, quoting Nicole Muchnik, "Le M.L.F., C'est toi, c'est moi," *Le Nouvel Observateur*, 27 August 1973.

20. *Oeuvres Complètes* (Geneva: Slatkine Reprints, 1975), p. 33. All quotations are from this edition, a reprinting of the Lausanne 1948 edition. Page numbers indicated in the text.

21. See Gayatri C. Spivak's introduction to her translation of Derrida's *Of Grammatology* (Baltimore: Johns Hopkins University Press, 1974), especially pp. xvii–xviii.

Chapter Six

1. Breton, *Anthologie de l'humour noir,* p. 219.

2. Guillaume Apollinaire, *"L'Enchanteur pourrissant" suivi des "Mamelles de Tirésias" et "Couleur du Temps"* (Paris: Gallimard, 1972), p. 131.

3. Raymond Roussel, *L'Etoile au front* (Paris: Pauvert, 1963), p. 40.

4. Jean Cocteau, *Les Mariés de la Tour Eiffel* (Paris: La Nouvelle Revue Française, 1924), p. 18 (Preface).

5. Ibid., p. 17.

6. Tzara, *Le Coeur à Gaz* (Paris: GLM 1946), p. 14.

7. *King Ubu,* Act IV, scene v.

8. Tzara, *Lampisteries précédées des Sept Manifestes Dada* (Paris: Pauvert, 1963), p. 74.

9. Ibid., p. 49.

10. *Oeuvres complètes,* Pléiade edition, p. 704.

11. Georges Ribemont-Dessaignes, *Théâtre* (Paris: Gallimard, 1966), p. 11.

12. Ibid., p. 200.

13. Antonin Arnaud, *Oeuvres complètes* (Paris: Gallimard, 1970), 1:343.

14. Green, *Tragic,* pp. 15–16.

15. Martin Esslin, *The Theater of the Absurd,* p. 313.

16. Ibid.

17. Sharon Spencer, *Space, Time, and Structure in the Modern Novel* (New York: New York University Press, 1971), p. xiv.

18. Jonathan Culler, *Ferdinand de Saussure* (New York: Penguin, 1977), pp. 126, 128.

19. Anaïs Nin, *The Novel of the Future* (New York: Collier Books, 1968), p. 171.

20. Ibid., p. 173.

21. David Lodge, "Historicism and Literary History: Mapping the Modern Period," *New Literary History* 10, no. 3 (Spring 1979):149–50.

22. Dina Sherzer, "Serial Construction in the Nouveau Roman," *Poetics Today* 1, no. 3 (1980):87.

23. Stephen Heath, *The Nouveau Roman* (Philadelphia: Temple University Press, 1972), p. 22.

24. *Faustroll,* in *Oeuvres complètes,* Pléiade edition, p. 669.

25. *Film Form,* ed. and tr. Jay Leyda (New York: Harcourt, Brace and World, 1949), pp. 37, 60.

26. *L'Amour absolu,* in *Oeuvres complètes,* Pléiade edition, p. 950.

27. Jean-Paul Sartre, *Situations* (Paris: Gallimard, 1947), 1:56–57.

28. The relationship between vital and sexual processes and symbolic formation is discussed at length in Jean Laplanche, *Vie et mort en psychanalyse* (Paris: Flammarion, 1970), pp. 17–43.

29. Laplanche presents Freud's often-revised definitions of the relationship between the death instinct and the pleasure principle, ibid., pp. 145–63.

30. *Faustroll,* in *Oeuvres complètes,* Pléiade edition, p. 668.

31. Ibid., p. 725.

32. Pléiade edition, p. 743.

33. *Faustroll,* Pléiade edition, p. 726.

34. Hugh Kenner proposes a theory of how the notion of "closed field" may apply to fiction in "Art in Closed Fields," *Virginia Quarterly Review* 30 (Autumn 1962):600.

35. Nin, *Novel of the Future,* p. 192.

Chapter Seven

1. "Reflections on Literature in Contemporary France," tr. Bruno Braunrot, *New Literary History* 10, no. 3 (Spring 1979):528.

2. Ibid., p. 531.

3. Leo Bersani, *Baudelaire and Freud* (Berkeley: University of California Press, 1977), p. 3.

4. We are concerned here with describing signs of narcissism in the text and not Jarry as a clinical case. Psychoanalysis provides a tool for practical literary criticism and a basis for understanding how lit-

erature operates. The analytic stance, by revealing the primitive material in the text and by providing a model for the sophisticated aspects of experience as well, is extremely helpful to the critic.

5. Otto Kernberg, *Borderline Conditions and Pathological Narcissism* (New York: Jason Aronson 1975), pp. 323, 230, 228, 233, 260, 264, 276, 316.

6. Jacques Lacan, *Ecrits* (Paris: Seuil, 1966), p. 95.

7. Leo Bersani, "The Subject of Power," *Diacritics,* Fall 1977, p. 19.

8. Kernberg, *Borderline,* p. 17.

9. Vamik D. Volkan, M.D., *Primitive Internalized Object Relations* (New York: International Universities Press, 1976), pp. 241, 239, 248, 318, 251, 319.

10. Christopher Lasch, "The Narcissist Society," *New York Review of Books,* 30 September 1976, p. 10.

11. Ibid., pp. 12–13.

12. This is discussed at length in his *The Restoration of the Self.*

13. Julia Kristeva, *La Révolution du langage poétique* (Paris: Seuil, 1974), p. 203.

14. Jacques Lacan, *Le Séminaire,* Livre I (Paris: Seuil 1975), p. 298.

15. J. Laplanche and J.-B. Pontalis, *The Language of Psychoanalysis,* tr. Donald Nicholson-Smith (New York: Norton, 1973), p. 210.

16. Gregory Ulmer, "The Discourse of the Imaginary," *Diacritics,* Spring 1980, p. 69.

17. Michel Foucault, *The Order of Things* (New York: Vintage Books, 1970), p. 49.

18. Ibid., pp. 49, 26–27, 385.

Selected Bibliography

PRIMARY SOURCES

1. Editions

Oeuvres complètes (8 volumes). Lausanne, Monte-Carlo: Henri Kaeser, 1948.

Oeuvres complètes. t. I, textes établis, présentés et annotés par Michel Arrivé. Paris: Gallimard, Bibliothèque de la Pléiade, 1972.

Le Manoir enchanté et quatre autres oeuvres inédites, présentées par Noël Arnaud. Paris: La Table Ronde, 1974.

2. Translations

The Garden of Priapus. Translated by Louis Coleman with notes and introduction by Matthew Josephson. Illustrated by Arthur Zaidenberg. [n.p.]. Reprint New York: Black Hawk Press, 1936.

Ubu Roi. Translated and Preface by Barbara Wright. London: Gaberbocchus Press, 1951.

King Turd. Translated by Beverly Keith and George Legman. New York: Boar's Head Books, 1953. Contains *King Turd, King Turd Enslaved,* and *Turd Cuckolded.*

Selected Works. Edited by Roger Shattuck and Simon Watson Taylor. London: Methuen, 1965. Contains Cyril Connolly's *Ubu Cuckolded,* Simon Watson-Taylor's *Faustroll.*

The Supermale, a Modern Novel. Translated by Barbara Wright. London: Jonathan Cape, 1968.

The Ubu Plays. Edited and Introduction by Simon Watson-Taylor. New York: Grove Press, 1969. Contains *Ubu Rex,* translated by C. Connolly and S. Watson-Taylor; *Ubu Cuckolded,* translated by C. Connolly; *Ubu Enchained,* translated by S. Watson-Taylor.

Caesar-Antichrist. Translated and Introduction by James Bierman. Tucson, Ariz.: Omen Press, 1971.

Ubu Rex. Translated by David Copelin. Vancouver: Pulp Press, 1973. An English-Canadian version.

SECONDARY SOURCES

1. Bibliography

Sutton, L. F. "An Evaluation of the Studies on Alfred Jarry from 1894–1963." Ph.D. dissertation, University of North Carolina at Chapel Hill, 1970.

2. Books

Arnaud, Noel. *Alfred Jarry, d'Ubu Roi au Docteur Faustroll.* Paris: La Table Ronde, 1974. A masterful, extremely detailed, and well-documented biography; this first volume covers 1891–1898, with numerous flashbacks; essential reading.

Arrivé, Michel. *Les langages de Jarry; essai de sémiotique littéraire.* Paris: Klinckseick, 1972. Fascinating semiotic study largely devoted to the Ubu "intertext": *Ubu Roi, Ubu Enchaîné, César-Antechirst.*

————. *Lire Jarry.* Brussels: Editions Complexe, 1976. Collection of articles, including an ingenious analysis of the sexual isotopie (from a Freudian perspective of sadism and masochism) and of the split between textual denotative and connotative levels.

Behar, Henri, *Jarry Dramaturge.* Paris: Nizet, 1980. (Incorporates *Le Monstre et la Marionnette.* Paris: Larousse, 1973.) An intelligent analysis of Jarry's dramaturgy, this study establishes the permanence of Ubu and of Jarry in modern theater.

Caradec, François. *A la Recherche d'Alfred Jarry.* Paris: Seghers, 1974. An insightful "life and works" book; chronological study emphasizing two major influences: Celtic or Breton tradition and schoolboy antics.

Chassé, Charles. *Dans les coulisses de la gloire: d'Ubu Roi au douanier Rousseau.* Paris: Nouvelle Revue Critique, 1947. This polemic on authorship of *Ubu Roi* offers useful documentation of activities of the students at the Rennes Lycée.

Chauveau, Paul. *Alfred Jarry; ou la naissance, la vie et la mort du Père Ubu, avec leurs portraits.* Paris: Mercure de France, 1932. Anecdotes not distinguished from facts, but presents some important first-hand accounts.

Cooper, Judith. *Ubu Roi: An Analytic Study.* New Orleans: Tulane Studies in Romance Languages and Literature, Number 6, 1974.

One of the only critical works in English, studies plot, the comic type, and especially Ubu's language.

Labelle, Maurice. *Alfred Jarry, Nihilism and the Theater of the Absurd.* New York: New York University Press, 1980. While rich in historical detail and plot summaries (such as are possible with Jarry) textual analyses are meager, superficial, and faulty. Tedious overuse of metonymy and certain vocabulary. Erroneously claims to be the first comprehensive study of Jarry in English; mostly treats dramaturgy.

Lebois, André. *Alfred Jarry l'irremplaçable.* Paris: Le Cercle du Livre, 1950. Methodical early study of works in chronological order; first real attempt to describe style.

Levesque, Jacques-Henri. *Alfred Jarry.* Paris: Seghers, 1951. Informative but very personal (sympathetic) early study; little new research.

Rachilde (pseud.). *Alfred Jarry; ou le Surmâle des lettres.* Paris: B. Grasset, 1928. A vivacious, sympathetic, anecdotal biography by Jarry's close friend.

Shattuck, Roger. *The Banquet Years.* New York: Random House, 1955. ("Suicide by Hallucination": pp. 187–222; "Poet and Pataphysician": pp. 223–54.) Excellent introduction to Jarry and his works. Sensitive and erudite study of "life and times" and of Pataphysics.

Stillman, Linda K. *La Théâtralité dans l'oeuvre d'Alfred Jarry.* York, S.C.: French Literature Publications Company, Inc., 1980. Analysis of theatrical elements in drama and prose; studies Jarry's novels, and his major doubles, in terms of theatricality.

Index

Adamov, Arthur, 125, 131
Alfred Jarry (LaBelle), 112
Amours jaunes, Les (Corbière), 1
Antaeus myth, 122–23
Anthologie de l'humour noir (Breton), 12, 35
Apollinaire, Guillaume, 11, 125–26, 131
Aristotle, 136
Arnaud, Noël, 7, 62, 80
Arrivé, Michel, 58, 60
L'Art littéraire, 6
Artaud, Antonin, 61, 124–25, 130

Barthes, Roland, 139
Bâton-à-Physique, 30–33, 45–46, 58, 67, 86, 115, 117–18, 144
Baudelaire, Charles, 139
Baudelaire and Freud (Bersani), 139
Beardsley, Aubrey, 22
Beaumont, Mme Leprince de, 57
Beckett, Samuel, 125
Belaval, Yvon, 58
Bergson, Henri, 4, 13, 51–52, 60
Bersani, Leo, 139
Blanchot, Maurice, 63

Boeuf sur le toit, Le (Cocteau), 126–27
Bonnard, Pierre, 12, 15
Bourreau de Péru, Le (Ribemont-Dessaignes), 128
Boys, Charles Vernon, 21–22
Breton, André, 12, 35, 52–53, 92, 127, 129

Cahiers du Collège de 'Pataphysique, 41
Canard Sauvage, Le, 13
Carroll, Lewis, 18
Chants de Maldoror, Les (Lautréamont), 32, 60, 63, 64, 79
Chasseguet-Smirgel, Janine, 72
Cocteau, Jean, 36, 126–27
Coeur à gaz, Le (Tzara), 127
Collière, Marcel, 11
Confessions of an Opium Eater (de Quincy), 65
Corbière, Tristan, 1
Courrière, Barthes de, 7
Cravan, Arthur, 125
Culler, Jonathan, 132

Dadaism, 124–25, 127–29
Daumal, René, 129
de Quincy, Thomas, 65
Derrida, Jacques, 39–40

Dossiers, 41
Double, A Psychoanalytic Study, The (Rank), 75
Douglas, Lord, 8
Dubillard, Roland, 125
Dürer, Albrecht, 7

L'Echo de Paris, 5, 6
Einstein, Albert, 135
Eisenstein, Sergei, 133
L'Empereur de Chine (Ribemont-Dessaignes), 127–28
Esslin, Martin, 130, 131
L'Etoile au front (Roussel), 126
Europe, 42

Fargue, Léon-Paul, 4, 9, 15, 61–62, 67, 81
Faust (Goethe), 27
Fénéon, Félix, 15
Figaro, 13
Foucault, Michel, 147–48
Franc-Nohain, 5, 22, 23, 26
Freud, Sigmund, 48, 52–53, 61, 77, 97, 114, 117, 125, 130, 132, 133, 135, 139, 145, 146

Gargantua (Rabelais), 25
Gauguin, Paul, 22
Gemini myth, 73–74
Ghelderode, Michel de, 131
Gide, André, 5, 36
Gidoville, 44–46, 48, 50, 56, 72, 92
Gilbert Lecomte, Roger, 129
Gillibert, Jean, 58, 77
Goethe, von, Johann, 27
Goll, Yvan, 128–29
Gourmont, Rémy de, 6, 7

Grabbe, Christian, 13
Green, André, 75, 95, 130

Hébert, Félix, 3, 17, 43, 48
Heisenberg, Werner, 37
Heraldry, 17, 29, 31–32, 72, 80, 98, 121, 147
Hérold, A. F., 11
Hugo, Victor, 2
Humor, 25, 46, 51–55, 84, 108–10, 124–25, 129–30

Ibsen, Henrik, 27, 116
Ionesco, Eugene, 125, 130
Intertextuality, 43–44, 77, 90, 139, 148

Jarry, Alfred, life and times, 1–15

WORKS:
"l'Acte unique," 6, 60
Almanach du Père Ubu, 12, 13
L'Amour absolu, 12, 63, 74, 76, 82, 90, 92–100, 101, 111, 115, 116, 144, 147
L'Amour en visites, 11, 77, 82, 85, 87, 88, 103, 108–10
Antiaclastes, Les, 43
"L'art et la science," 43
Au Paradis ou le Vieux de la Montagne, 82, 88–91, 117
L'autre Alceste, 76, 78–82, 85, 86, 104, 117
"Bataille de Morsang, La," 111, 121
"Battre les femmes," 102–103
Bidasse et Compagnie, 43
César-Antechrist, 6, 17, 29–34, 45, 46, 58, 60, 66,

72, 82, 83, 88, 95, 98,
118, 121, 135, 137, 144
Chandelle verte, La, 13
"Chez la Muse," 82, 85–88
"Chez la Vieille Dame," 7,
77, 109
"Commentaire pour servir à la
construction pratique de la
machine à explorer le
temps," 12–13, 38, 137
Dragonne, La, 14, 111–23,
143, 144
Etre et Vivre, 6, 95
"Gestes," 13
*Gestes et opinions du docteur
Faustroll, pataphysicien,* 6,
11, 12, 17, 18–29, 30,
37, 41, 55, 77, 90, 100,
111, 116, 127, 128, 134,
135, 136–37, 141, 143,
145, 147
"Guignol," 6, 16–17, 45
Haldernablou, 6–7, 60–64,
66, 67, 78–79, 82, 85,
87, 88, 92, 113, 143, 144,
145
Jours et les Nuits, Les, 6, 7, 8,
11, 17, 24, 56, 61, 65–
78, 79, 87, 89, 90, 97,
133, 141, 142
"Linteau," 17
Messaline, 13, 104–107, 135,
143
Minutes de sable mémorial, Les,
6, 7, 16–17, 60–64, 74,
85–86, 87, 90, 109, 111
Moutardier du pape, Le, 13
L'Objet aimé, 76, 107–108
Ontogénie, 2, 43
"Opium," 7, 80, 153n11

Pantagruel, 11, 14
Papesse Jeanne, La, 14
"Paralipomena of Ubu, The,"
44, 45, 79
Par la taille, 11, 13
Perhinderion, 8
Peur chez l'Amour, La, 82–84
Polonais, Les, 49
"Questions about Theater,"
11, 57, 59
Revenge of Night, The, 76–77,
82, 86, 87
Silènes, Les, 13
"Speculations," 13
Surmâle, Le, 10, 13, 24, 25–
26, 59, 63, 67, 82, 84,
100–104, 105, 108, 120,
128, 133, 140–41, 142,
144, 145
Ubu cocu, 43, 45, 47, 48, 56,
107, 112, 134
Ubu Enchaîné, 12, 36, 45, 47,
56, 66, 94
Ubu Roi, 3, 6, 8, 10–15, 22,
24, 28, 31, 45, 47, 48,
49–58, 72, 73, 120–21
Ubu sur la butte, 13, 49
"Visions actuelles et futures,"
83
L'Ymagier, 6, 7, 8, 29

Jarry, Anselme (father), 1–2,
114
Jarry, Caroline Q. (mother), 1,
2, 4
Jarry, Charlotte (sister), 2, 111,
123
Joyce, James, 136
Jung, Carl, 27–28, 59, 102,
112, 114

Kahn, Gustave, 5, 8
Kelvin, Lord, 22, 28
Kernberg, Otto, 140, 145
Kevil, Hunter, 48
Kohut, Heinz, 140, 141–42, 146
Kristeva, Julia, 147

LaBelle, Maurice, 112
Lacan, Jacques, 61, 142, 146–47
Lasch, Christopher, 140, 145
Lautréamont, 32, 60, 61, 63
Léautaud, Paul, 15
Lesteven, Louis, 35
Livre de la pitié et de la mort, Le (Loti), 77
Loti, Pierre, 77
Louys, Pierre, 5
Lugné-Poe, 3, 6, 8, 53

Mallarmé, Stéphane, 10, 22
Malthusalem (Goll), 128–29
Mammelles de Tirésias, Les (Apollinaire), 125–26
Manifesto of Monsieur aa the antiphilosopher (Tzara), 127
Mariés de la Tour Eiffel, Les (Cocteau), 126
Marinetti, Emilio, 124
Marx, Karl, 145
Mauriac, François, 135
Mendès, Catulle, 5
Mercure de France, 4, 5, 6, 12
Merdre, 46–49, 72, 119, 126, 151n8, 152n9
Mirbeau, Octave, 5, 15
Morin, Charles, 3
Morin, Henri, 3

Narcissism, 65, 68, 72, 75–76, 83, 113, 123, 140–48, 157n4
Natanson, Thadée, 13, 14
Nero, 41
Nietzsche, Friedrich, 4, 40, 125
Nin, Anaïs, 132, 138
Novel of the Future, The (Nin), 132, 138
Nulle Part, 55–56, 66, 119

Oedipal complex, 92, 95–96, 98–99, 146
L'Oeil, 13
Oral Sadism, 25, 49, 73, 93, 102–103, 105, 110, 117–18, 141, 143–44
Orestes, 96–97, 99

Pantagruel (Rabelais), 98
Parade (Cocteau), 126
Pataphysics, 6, 16–42, 46, 89, 101, 105, 119, 129–30, 137–38, 142, 147, 149n1
Peer Gynt (Ibsen), 27, 28, 116
Perpetual–Motion–Food, 102, 128, 140
Petits poèmes amorphes (Franc-Nohain), 23, 26
Phallic mother, 96–99, 107, 114–21, 144
Plato, 30
Plume, La, 13
Poe, Edgar Allan, 3, 52
Poesia, 13
Proust, Marcel, 36
Psychanalyse et critique littéraire (Clancier), 58
Puppetry, 26, 49–51, 56, 107, 131

Quernest, Charles Jean-Baptiste
    (grandfather), 114, 123
Quillard, Pierre, 11

Rabelais, François, 3, 25, 41,
    98
Rachilde (pseud.), 2, 9, 10, 12,
    15, 24, 118
Rank, Otto, 75, 76
Régnier, Henri de, 4
Revue blanche, 13, 78, 90
Rhoides, Emmanuel, 14
Ribemont-Dessaignes, Georges,
    125, 127–28
Rimbaud, Arthur, 1, 41, 114
Rousseau, Henri, 11
Roussel, Raymond, 41, 125–26,
    136

Sacqueville, Erbrand de, 114
Sade, Marquis de, 136
Saillet, Maurice, 13
Sainmont, J.-H., 61
Saison en enfer, Une (Rimbaud), 1
Saltas, Dr., 14
Sarlius, Léonard, 8
Sartre, Jean-Paul, 135
Scherz, Satire, Ironie und tiefere
    Bedeutung (Grabbe), 13
Schwob, Marcel, 5
Shakespeare, William, 3, 53
Socrates, 18
Sollers, Philippe, 136
Soupault, Philippe, 52

Spurs, Nietzsche's Styles (Derrida),
    40
Surrealism, 25, 56, 84, 104,
    124, 129–30

Terrasse, Claude, 14, 22, 28
Theater and Its Double, The (Ar-
    taud), 125
Theater of the Absurd, The,
    124–25, 130–31
Théâtre Alfred Jarry, 62, 125
Théâtre de l'Oeuvre, 3, 8, 27,
    56
Théâtre des Phynances, 3
Time Machine, The (Wells), 13,
    38
Tison-Braun, Micheline, 44
Todorov, Tvetan, 139
Torma, Julien, 41, 131
Tragic Effect, The (Green), 95
Tzara, Tristan, 125, 127

Vaché, Jacques, 125
Valéry, Paul, 5, 15
Vallette, Alfred, 5, 11, 14, 15,
    64
Vallette, Rachilde, 5, 11, 15
Vian, Boris, 131

Weingarten, Romain, 131
Wells, H. G., 13, 38
Wilde, Oscar, 8
William the Conqueror, 114

Zaessinger, Fanny, 8